TACTICAL HELICOPTER MISSIONS

ABOUT THE AUTHOR

Kevin Means learned to fly airplanes while attending high school and then joined the United States Navy in 1977. He spent four years as an Anti-Submarine Warfare Operator and Search and Rescue crewman aboard Kaman SH-2F helicopters and was assigned to helicopter squadron HSL-35 at Naval Air Station North Island.

Kevin remained in San Diego after his honorable discharge in 1981 and joined the San Diego Police Department. He worked as a patrol officer for five years; was assigned to the Border Crime Prevention Unit, whose mission was to prevent violent crime in the isolated canyon areas near the US/Mexican border; and was also a Narcotics and Gangs detective.

Kevin became a Tactical Flight Officer for the newly created San Diego Police Air Support Unit in 1989 and obtained his Commercial helicopter certificate in 1992. He is a Certified Flight Instructor in airplanes and helicopters and has logged more than 9000 hours of flight time. He is the unit's helicopter training officer, and is a night vision goggle check-airman and Tactical Flight Officer trainer.

Kevin has consulted with infrared manufacturers on the designs of their systems, and with other industries on the use of Night Vision Goggles and helicopter training procedures. He chaired the Education and Training Committee of the Airborne Law Enforcement Association and was the association's president from 2002 to 2003.

His wife, Cyndi Jo, is a Deputy District Attorney in San Diego, and they have two daughters, Erin Lynne and Andi Jo. They reside in Lakeside, California.

TACTICAL HELICOPTER MISSIONS

How to Fly Safe, Effective Airborne Law Enforcement Missions

By

KEVIN P. MEANS

With a Foreword by

Captain Jim Di Giovanna

Los Angeles County Sheriff's Department (Ret.)

CHARLES C THOMAS · PUBLISHER, LTD.
Springfield · Illinois · U.S.A.

Published and Distributed Throughout the World by

CHARLES C THOMAS • PUBLISHER, LTD.
2600 South First Street
Springfield, Illinois 62704

©2007 by CHARLES C THOMAS • PUBLISHER, LTD.

ISBN-13: 978-0-398-07738-9 (paper)
ISBN-10: 0-398-07738-X (paper)

Library of Congress Catalog Card Number: 2006101702

With THOMAS BOOKS *careful attention is given to all details of man-
ufacturing and design. It is the Publisher's desire to present books that are sat-
isfactory as to their physical qualities and artistic possibilities and appropri-
ate for their particular use.* THOMAS BOOKS *will be true to those laws
of quality that assure a good name and good will.*

Printed in the United States of America
CR-R-3

Library of Congress Cataloging-in-Publication Data

Means, Kevin P.
 Tactical helicopter missions : how to fly safe, effective airborne law
enforcement missions / by Kevin P. Means ; with a foreword by
Captain Jim Di Giovanna.
   p. cm.
 Includes index.
 ISBN-13: 978-0-398-07738-9 (paperbound)
 ISBN-10: 0-398-07738-X (paperbound)
 1. Aeronautics in police work. 2. Helicopters. I. Title.
 HV8080.A3M43 2007
 363.2'32--dc22
                                                    2006101702

This book is dedicated to my lovely wife, Cyndi Jo and to my wonderful daughters, Erin Lynne and Andi Jo, who have had to live with my addiction to airborne law enforcement for many years. It is also dedicated to Mom, Dad, Betty and Daryl who have always been there for me.

FOREWORD

Fifteen years ago, I first met Kevin Means through our mutual affiliation with the Airborne Law Enforcement Association. Immediately I was impressed with his professionalism, passion for airborne law enforcement, and hunger to learn of more effective and efficient ways of catching crooks from the air. I knew right away that we shared common interests: Aviation safety and professionalism, a strong desire to advance the mission and capabilities of airborne law enforcement, and taking great pleasure from putting bad guys in jail.

Since Kevin and I met, technology has played a major role in evolving the use and tactics of airborne law enforcement. Prior to 1990, and, of course, prior to the release of several hundred military surplus aircraft, airborne law enforcement outside of major metropolitan areas had not fully matured. In fact, very few agencies throughout the United States even had an aviation unit. Thermal imagery and night vision goggles were in limited use, traffic enforcement was one of the primary missions, and the air unit was always under the budget knife. Unfortunately, the latter fact hasn't changed.

Today, over 400 law enforcement agencies in the U.S. alone employ aviation units, with many more in Canada, Europe, and Australia. The technological evolution has advanced airborne tactics and placed greater emphasis on night vision devices, making thermal imagery a mainstay while expanding the use of night vision goggles in many urban cities. Now, with such technological advances, air unit tactics can focus more on force protection, crime suppression and suspect searches and captures, with vehicle pursuits being a primary air support mission. Multiband digital communications, moving maps, and GPS tracking devices all have greatly assisted in making air support an indispensable crime fighting resource.

In this book, Kevin captures the intricate nuances of the unique and specialized profession of airborne law enforcement. He successfully summarizes the tactical excellence needed to transform the science and technology of police air support into a masterful art.

Kevin's subject matter expertise comes after many successful years of experience as a tactical flight officer, pilot and flight instructor, along with some rather unsuccessful episodes of misinterpreted thermal images, losing crafty crooks, and enduring a few tough breaks, all of which served as valuable lessons. In writing this book, Kevin has shared each of these experiences, good and bad, and has provided a textbook by which all of us in this profession will benefit and become much better at what we do. For this, we are most grateful.

Captain Jim Di Giovanna
Los Angeles County Sheriff's Department, Retired

PREFACE

A well-trained aircrew that is proficient with their tactics, technology, and each other will significantly enhance the safety, efficiency, and effectiveness of officers on the ground. When an aircrew is overhead, providing patrol support, suspects are much less likely to continue their criminal activity or escape. The missions that aircrews perform, however, are only part of the equation; how they perform them is what makes the difference between an effective aircrew and one that is less effective. This book is about law enforcement helicopter tactics and strives to explain why certain tactics and procedures are safer and more effective than others.

It would be easy to use words like "right" and "wrong" when describing different tactics, but "safe" and "effective" are words that more accurately describe what we're trying to accomplish: the safe and successful completion of our missions.

Most law enforcement helicopters are equipped with similar tactical equipment, but the tactics of aviation units often vary, sometimes significantly. After years of studying the tactics of various agencies, it became apparent that in some cases, crewmembers performed missions a certain way for one reason: "Because we've always done it that way." Tactics were handed down from generation to generation and nothing ever changed—even with the acquisition of new technology.

It is unrealistic to assert that only one specific tactic would apply to all airborne law enforcement missions under all conditions. There are too many variables that might affect how a specific mission should be performed. The tactics described in this book, however, have proven to enhance the effectiveness, and in many cases the safety of aircrews and ground units. Some require a greater degree of crew coordination than others and a higher degree of technical proficiency, but the payoff is a safer and more effective aircrew.

ix

It is no secret that suspects study the tactics of law enforcement, including airborne law enforcement. Criminals are aware of thermal imagers and other airborne technology, so it is incumbent upon aircrews to employ tactics that make it difficult or impossible for suspects to defeat that technology.

The duties of pilots and Tactical Flight Officers have become technical in nature and can be very demanding. It is impossible to know what skills each reader has, but make no mistake about it, when an aircrew is proficient with their tactics, technology, and each other, they are much more likely to be safe and more effective.

K.P.M.

ACKNOWLEDGMENTS

Many airborne law enforcement professionals provided me with valuable insight into their operations, and it would be impossible to list them all. However, I would like to acknowledge and thank certain people who assisted me while researching this book: Officers Jack Schonely and Jim Weigh of the Los Angeles Police Air Support Unit, Sergeant Dave Douglas of the San Diego County Sheriff's ASTREA unit, George Dempsey of the Martin County Sheriff's Office Aviation Section, and Jeff Werblun of the Sacramento County Sheriff's Metro Air Bureau.

Many of the photos in this book were provided by some very talented photographers, including Glenn Grossman, Tony Zeljeznjak, and Dan Megna. Thank you very much for all of your help.

It is most important to acknowledge and thank the members of the San Diego Police Air Support Unit for their never ending patience and support. It is especially important to acknowledge the assistance of Officer Todd Jager who, for more than a decade, spent countless hours in helicopters with me evaluating, testing, and practicing the tactics and techniques described in this book.

CONTENTS

TACTICAL HELICOPTER MISSIONS

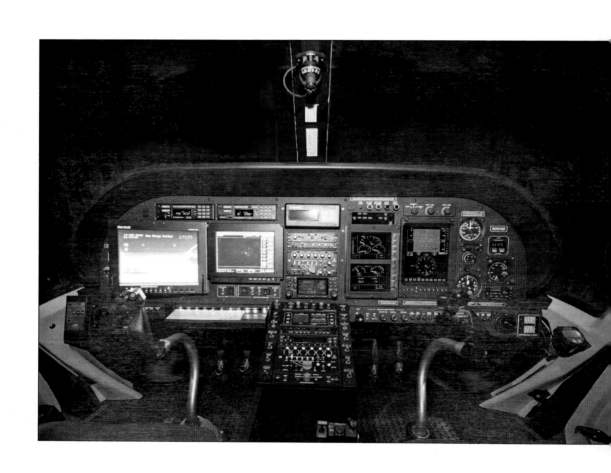

Chapter 1

CREW QUALIFICATIONS AND TACTICAL EQUIPMENT

CREW QUALIFICATIONS

Tactical Flight Officers

Helicopter cockpits have traditionally been designed with only the pilot in mind. In the early days of airborne law enforcement, the crewmember who sat next to the pilot was essentially a passenger with a badge. They were often referred to as "spotters" or "observers" or occasionally by less flattering titles such as "self-loading baggage" or "mindless light shiners." Their duties were generally limited to looking outside and telling ground units what they saw.

For the most part, those titles have been replaced with "Tactical Flight Officer" (TFO), a title which more accurately reflects the duties performed. Those duties are substantially more difficult than they were years ago. While it is still necessary for them to look outside and relay what they see, TFOs are also tasked with operating some very sophisticated equipment. They must work closely with pilots, monitor and operate multiple radios, operate and interpret thermal imagers, and coordinate the activities of ground units. They must be able to perform those duties quickly and effectively while applying good officer safety tactics during the day and night and oftentimes under intense pressure.

Some Law enforcement agencies rotate their TFOs in and out of the aviation unit with little understanding of how difficult their job can be, or how long it takes for them to become proficient. For the most part, that practice is a holdover from the early days of airborne law enforcement, when crewmembers simply looked outside and *observed*. Essentially, if they didn't get airsick, anyone could do that job. Today, however, it takes a dedicated individual a considerable amount of time, effort and skill to become a good Tactical Flight Officer.

When an agency creates an air support unit, they invest a significant amount of money in aircraft, training, and technology, and the TFO is the link between those expensive resources and the officers on the ground. If the TFO is not technically proficient, or cannot communicate effectively, or apply good officer safety tactics, the potential benefits of the aircrew will be lost.

Pilots

Pilots who fly airborne law enforcement missions can be civilians or sworn law enforcement personnel. Some feel that law enforcement officers have an advantage when flying certain missions, because their law enforcement experience gives them additional insight when assisting ground units.

No matter who flies the aircraft, the most important prerequisites are that they possess the necessary skills and qualifications and fly professionally. Professionalism equates to safety. Just as the TFO's duties have become more complex, so have those of the pilot. The integration of new technology affects not only how TFOs do their jobs, but how pilots fly missions.

Crew Seating Arrangements

Unlike police cars, crew seating arrangements in law enforcement helicopters differ significantly. The most common seating arrangement is right-seat pilot and left-seat TFO, but some airframe manufacturers build helicopters that are flown from the left seat.

There is no overwhelming benefit of either design, because the mathematics and tactics of flying missions are the same. However, the direction the aircraft turns when orbiting a call is immensely important to the overall effectiveness of the aircrew. The aircraft's seating arrangement is the primary factor to consider when determining which direction to orbit.

To be as effective as possible, pilots flying from the right seat must turn to the left when orbiting calls, and pilots flying from the left seat must turn to the right. Orbiting calls in this manner is safer and more effective because both crewmembers will have a better view of the aircraft's instruments and direction of flight, as well as the tactical environment and tactical displays.

These concepts are explained in-depth throughout this book. Can an aircrew ignore this recommendation and reverse the direction of their orbits? Yes, and they can even operate safely when doing so, but they will not be as effective as they could be. Remember, the goal is to be safe and effective.

The Tactical Environment

The term "tactical environment" is used throughout this book and refers to the location of a call or incident. In residential areas, for example, the tactical environment is the area around the house where the call originated. It is the area where suspects will likely be, or where activity related to an incident is likely to occur.

The size of a tactical environment will vary, depending on the type of call. If it is a traffic stop, for example, the tactical environment will be relatively small. If it is a foot pursuit through a shopping mall, however, it is going to be much larger.

TACTICAL EQUIPMENT

Airborne law enforcement has experienced a technological revolution. Missions that used to be flown with only a searchlight and a police radio are now flown with thermal imagers, night vision goggles, and a variety of advanced avionics and sensors. Certain pieces of equipment have become standard in the industry and almost mandatory for effective airborne law enforcement operations.

Some of the most common technology found in law enforcement helicopters is discussed in this book. The use of that technology, in conjunction with good law enforcement skills, tactics, and judgment, are what enables an aircrew to provide effective air support to officers.

Forward Looking Infrared (FLIR)

Most law enforcement helicopters are equipped with Forward Looking Infrared (FLIR–also known as thermal imagers). No single piece of equipment has had the same impact on airborne law enforcement as FLIR. Thermal imagers have revolutionized an aircrew's ability to search, even in total darkness. They enable aircrews to search from higher altitudes and are tactically more effective than searchlights during most nighttime searches.

A large portion of this book deals with thermal imaging missions because those missions require specific technical skills, unique tactics, and good crew coordination skills in order for the aircrew to be as effective as possible.

An important component of a thermal imager is the monitor. The FLIR monitor must be large enough for both crewmembers to see it, and it must be installed efficiently. It should be mounted in front of the TFO, but the pilot must also have a clear view of it. Figure 1 is an instrument panel in a Bell 206, and Figure 2 is an instrument panel in a MD 500. The monitors are on opposite sides of the panels, because

Figure 1. The FLIR monitor is on the left side of this Bell 206 instrument panel, directly in front of the TFO. The monitor is also visible to the pilot.

the seating arrangements in those aircraft are reversed. In both examples, however, the monitors are visible to both crewmembers.

Most law enforcement helicopters are equipped with a single monitor to display images from a FLIR, a video camera, a moving map and perhaps a computer. Typically, the TFO switches between sources to view the most pertinent information. Dual monitors, however, minimize the need to do this and provide the aircrew with much more information, simultaneously. Figures 3 and 4 are examples of dual-monitor installations. Figure 3 is a picture of a Bell OH-58 instrument panel, and Figure 4 is a picture of an American Eurocopter AS 350 instrument panel.

Figure 2. In this MD 500 the TFO sits in the right seat, but both crewmembers have clear view of the monitor.

Searchlights

Another common piece of equipment is the searchlight. These generally range in power from 5 to 30 million candlepower. They are often referred to as spotlights because their primary use is often not to search, but to illuminate things on the ground for officers.

Before FLIR, searchlights were indeed searchlights. They were used by themselves or in combination with binoculars to search in dark areas. Searchlights are still in regular use, but they are not nearly as effective as FLIR for most types of nighttime searches. They are effective, however, when searching for people in the water. Visible light penetrates water better than infrared energy, so it is usually easier to see someone struggling in the surf, for example, if the aircrew is using a searchlight.

Figure 3: This is a Bell OH-58 equipped with dual monitors. The TFO sits in the left seat, but both monitors are visible to both crewmembers. This configuration provides the aircrew with more information, simultaneously.

When searching for missing children at night, the aircrew should initially scan all the swimming pools in the area with a searchlight. If a child has fallen into a pool, a FLIR will not be able to detect them if they are submerged. The light from the searchlight, however, will penetrate the water much better than the child's infrared energy, which will make it easier for the aircrew to see them.

Searchlights can also be used tactically to throw suspicion off an aircrew's true mission. People on the ground cannot see where the FLIR is pointed, but they can see where the searchlight is pointed. An aircrew can use this to their advantage on certain missions.

Figure 4: This is an American Eurocopter AS 350 cockpit with dual monitors. Both monitors are located in front of the TFO, but both crewmembers can see them.

Global Positioning System (GPS) Maps

Global Positioning System (GPS) maps, also known as "moving maps," have become the standard for airborne law enforcement operations when navigating to calls. The days of a TFO holding a penlight in their mouth to read from a paper map book are not completely gone, but that process has certainly been eclipsed by new, more efficient technology. Moving maps are not difficult to use but there are some techniques that an aircrew can employ to use them more efficiently.

Binoculars

There are two types of binoculars: stabilized and unstabilized. Stabilized binoculars work better in helicopters, especially when the TFO is trying to read street signs or addresses. There are different methods of stabilization: gyro and electronic. Gyrostabilization seems to work better over a wider range of movement, but gyro-stabilized binoculars are usually more expensive to purchase and tend to be less reliable.

Electronically stabilized binoculars are usually more reliable, but they do not stabilize an image as well. They also have the advantage of being smaller and lighter, which makes them less fatiguing to use and easier to store in space-limited cockpits.

Both kinds of binoculars require a power supply and most have the option of using external power from the aircraft or internal power from batteries. When possible, they should be powered with external power from the aircraft, because it is only a matter of time before someone forgets to replace the batteries and they die—right when they are needed most.

Public Address Systems

Public Address (PA) systems can be very useful when trying to communicate with the public, and it is worth taking some time to explain some of their uses and limitations.

When officers interview witnesses at crime scenes, they broadcast the suspect's description for other officers in the area. Sometimes there are witnesses nearby who have valuable information but they do not know it, because they do not know what the police are looking for. They may have seen the suspect get into a car or change clothes, or the suspect might be standing right next to them.

There are some important tactical and safety issues that aircrews need to consider before making PA announcements. For example, some PA systems are more effective than others and the pilot can fly outside the aircraft's height-velocity (HV) curve when using them. Other PA systems require that the aircraft be flown inside or near the HV curve for people to understand what is being said. If that is the case, the aircrew needs to evaluate the risk/benefit ratio carefully. For example, is it daytime or nighttime, and how long ago did the crime occur? Is the suspect a ten-year-old boy who stole a neighbor's skateboard, or an armed robbery suspect who was just seen in the area? Are there people nearby who might have seen the suspect, or is the area largely uninhabited? Is the environment below the aircraft a downtown highrise district, a business complex, or a residential area? What is the wind's direction and velocity?

If the aircraft's PA system requires that the helicopter must operate low level, aircrews should avoid the practice of automatically making PA announcements simply because they have been requested to do so. Risk management must play an important role in their decision-making process.

Another thing to consider is gunfire. A surprising number of law enforcement helicopters and crewmembers have been hit by gunfire, and several have crashed or have been forced to land. What better target for a suspect with a rifle than a law enforcement helicopter hovering, or flying low and slow making PA announcements? In many cases the aircrew might not know they are being shot at, because they might not be able to hear the gunfire. Figure 5 is a picture of a MD 500 tail rotor blade that was hit by an unknown caliber of bullet. The aircrew was searching for a robbery suspect and the helicopter was flying at approximately 50 knots, at about 500 feet AGL. They never heard the gunshot, and the only thing they felt was a momentary shudder in the airframe.

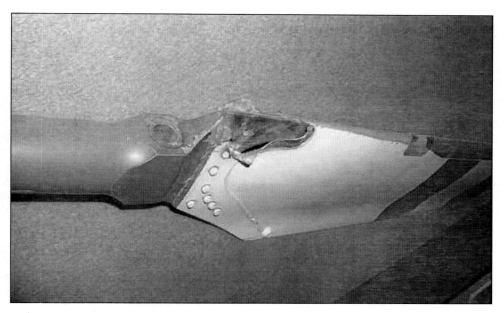

Figure 5: This tail rotor blade from a MD 500 was hit by an unknown caliber firearm while the aircraft was flying at approximately 500 feet AGL.

Kites are another hazard to be aware of when flying low level, but kites can also be found at amazingly high altitudes. Figure 6 is a picture of some monofilament kite string that became entangled in the helicopter's swash plate assembly and pitch change links. The aircraft hit the kite string in the late afternoon at about 500 feet AGL. Neither crewmember saw the kite, nor did they realize that they had hit the string until after they landed. Fortunately, the damage was minor. When flying low level for any reason, aircrews should be vigilant for kites that may be above them, as well as in front of them.

Figure 6: The monofilament kite string in this picture became entangled in the helicopter's swash plate assembly and pitch change links when the aircraft flew under a kite.

Some PA systems are easier to understand than others and most are very directional. The speakers have to be aimed toward the audience for people to understand what is being said. The TFO will likely have to make multiple announcements while the aircraft orbits to ensure that people on the ground hear the message.

If the decision has been made to make PA announcements, the TFO needs to get accurate information before the pilot descends. From a safety perspective, it makes no sense to fly at a less safe altitude and airspeed if the aircrew has not received the most accurate information available. From a tactical perspective, the PA announcements are not likely to be very effective if the aircrew is broadcasting the wrong information.

If the aircrew is asked to make PA announcements for a child who is missing from his or her home, for example, they should insist that an officer go to the child's home first and confirm that the child is missing. They also need to confirm the child's name and clothing description. Oftentimes, children are not missing at all. They are at home sleeping, or hiding, or they have returned home, but no one informed the police.

When making PA announcements for missing people, or for suspects who may be in the area, the message needs to be clear and concise. Example:

The police department is looking for a bank robbery suspect who was last seen in this area. He's a twenty-five-year-old white male, last seen wearing a black jacket, blue jeans and white tennis shoes. If anyone has seen him, please contact an officer, or dial 911.

The TFO should use as few words as possible and should repeat the message several times while the aircraft orbits. The sound of the TFO's voice is going to be moving across the ground as the aircraft moves. If the TFO takes too long to broadcast the information, the sound pattern will travel past people on the ground before they hear the entire message. This affects some PA systems more than others. The wind direction is another thing to consider, because sound tends to be carried in the direction the wind is blowing.

It is remarkable how often initial suspect descriptions from a dispatcher are wrong, but it is not surprising. When victims are confronted by suspects, it is a stressful situation and they often overlook obvious details. Occasionally, important details get lost or changed in the communications process, so it is very important for an officer to go to the scene first and contact the witness. Sometimes the TFO has to tactfully remind officers that someone needs to go to the scene to get accurate information for everyone.

When the TFO is making PA announcements, both crewmembers should be looking outside for the suspect and for witnesses. Witnesses may hear the announcements and realize that they saw the suspect. They often try to get the aircrew's attention by waving at the helicopter. If the aircrew sees someone doing that, the pilot needs to position the helicopter so the PA speakers are pointed toward them. The TFO should use the PA system to tell the witnesses that they see them, and then tell the witnesses to point in the direction they last saw the suspect. Example:

> *I'm speaking to the man in the red shirt on the sidewalk who is waving at the helicopter. If you saw the suspect, point in the direction you last saw him.*

The TFO then needs to have an officer contact that witness immediately. It is better to have an officer contact the witness than to have the witness call the police, because it is usually more expeditious and there is less chance of miscommunication. If the aircrew believes from the witness's actions that they saw the suspect, and it seems reasonable, they should focus their attention in that area and notify the ground units.

A perimeter should already have been established, but the TFO may need to remind officers not to leave their perimeter positions. The perimeter may have to be expanded or modified, based on information from the witness.

Experienced aircrews can often tell when something looks out of place, or when someone is acting in a legitimate or a suspicious manner. This valuable insight is based on experience, but until the aircrew gets specific details from the witness, they are only operating on assumptions.

Suspects often change clothes after committing crimes and the description the TFO is broadcasting may not be accurate, but it is still the best information available. Maybe a witness saw the suspect take off his jacket, or a witness may have seen the suspect get into a car. Witnesses probably are not going to realize that they saw something important, and no one is going to know what they saw unless someone communicates with them.

Night Vision Goggles

Night vision goggles (NVGs) are used by aircrews when flying in dark environments, but they can also be used when flying over well-lit cities. It is often possible to see suspects moving through alleys and other dark areas that are not visible with the naked eye. It is also much easier for pilots to see obstructions and other hazards in dark lots, schoolyards, and fields.

NVGs are very effective when flying in dark environments, but they do have limitations. For example, they do not work well in total darkness, especially in low-contrast environments. They have a limited field of view (40 degrees), and incompatible cockpit lighting significantly affects their performance. NVGs are not a substitute for FLIR, because they do not resolve heat contrast well enough to detect hiding suspects under most conditions. NVGs and FLIR are not competing technologies, they are augmenting technologies.

NVGs not only increase safety, they also provide the aircrew with some tactical advantages when used with other equipment. For example, the latest generation of thermal imagers can be equipped with infrared laser pointers. These lasers are not visible to the naked eye and can only be seen when viewed with NVGs or similar night vision technology. This feature gives the aircrew a tremendous advantage when trying to point out the location of a hiding suspect to ground units. If the ground units have some kind of night vision technology, they can see where the laser is pointed, because it is bore-sighted to the FLIR. Suspects will not know when the laser is pointed at them, because they cannot see it.

Even if ground units do not have night vision capabilities, the laser is still helpful if the pilot is using NVGs. For example, when the FLIR operator has found a suspect in a large canyon, it can sometimes be difficult to determine exactly where the suspect is if there are no landmarks nearby. When the suspect is lazed, however, the pilot can look outside with NVGs and see exactly where the suspect is hiding. This makes it easier for them to orbit the tactical environment, and it is easier for the TFO to direct ground units to the suspect.

Chapter 2

RESPONDING TO CALLS

PATROL PHILOSOPHIES

Many agencies have air support units with scheduled patrol shifts and their aircrews respond to calls from the air. Others wait until they are called out and respond from the ground. A variety of factors will dictate how an aircrew responds, but there is no question which method is more effective. For patrol support the helicopter needs to be in the air to be as effective as possible. Many law enforcement calls last only a few minutes. If the aircrew has to respond from the ground the incident might be over before they even get in the air. A law enforcement helicopter does no one any good when it is sitting on the ground.

Police cars have distinctive markings, because their high-profile presence deters criminal activity. They patrol various parts of a city in direct proportion to the amount of criminal activity in an area. Officers do not sit at police stations waiting to be dispatched, because the agency loses the crime deterrent benefit of having police cars visible in the community, and their response time would be much greater. That patrol philosophy is identical for effective air support.

From a risk management perspective, responding to urgent calls from the ground can put enormous pressure on an aircrew to rush, and people are more likely to make mistakes when they are in a hurry. More than one aircrew has started a helicopter with the main rotor blades tied down, and aircrews are more likely to overlook checklist items when they are in a hurry.

TFO'S–MONITORING THE RADIOS

When an aircrew is on patrol and not en route to a call, they can minimize their chances of missing important calls by setting up their radios properly. Most large agencies that have air support also have separate radio frequencies for different geographical regions in their jurisdiction. The helicopter should be equipped with two of the agency's radios. One of them should be designated as the primary radio and it should be clear which radio that is.

During normal operations, the primary radio should only be used to monitor one frequency: the frequency of the area the aircrew is patrolling, or the frequency of the area they are en route to. When the aircrew gets dispatched to a call on another frequency, the TFO should switch the primary radio to that frequency. The second radio should be scanning the agency's other dispatch frequencies and its volume should be set lower than the primary radio.

If the aircrew has the ability to monitor other agencies on different radios, the volumes of those radios should be set even lower or at least set differently than the primary and secondary radios. This volume differential helps the aircrew identify on which radio a call was dispatched. This technique does not eliminate the possibility of missing a call, nor does it identify what frequency a call was dispatched on, but it helps.

When working a low-priority call, some TFOs choose to focus their attention only on the call at hand and not monitor the other radios. There is nothing necessarily wrong with this, but in many cases, it is not the most efficient use of the radios or of the TFO's time.

If the call being worked is a low priority call, for example, which appears to be under control, it is reasonable to expect an experienced TFO to listen to other frequencies. If they do not monitor the other frequencies, they might miss an urgent call elsewhere. Aircrews should not rely on dispatchers to call them, because it might take a dispatcher a few moments to deal with an urgent call before he/she has a chance to request air support. The aircrew will be able to respond faster if they hear the call themselves. If the aircrew is already working an urgent call, however, the TFO should consider not monitoring the other radios. They can be distracting and may cause the TFO to miss something important.

To enhance safety of flight, TFOs should be monitoring the aircraft radio when the helicopter is taking off or landing at an airport. The chances of a mid-air collision increase significantly near airports, so both crewmembers need to be looking outside for other aircraft and listening to position reports from other pilots and controllers.

NEW TACTICAL FLIGHT OFFICERS

A helicopter cockpit is a noisy, cramped, and complex learning environment, and some TFOs are going to demonstrate the ability to monitor the radios better than others. When training new TFOs, the trainer should not overload the TFO with too many tasks too soon. During their initial training, TFOs should be encouraged to listen to all the law enforcement radios while on patrol, but they should only be allowed to monitor the primary radio when working a call.

The process of learning how to monitor several radios and the process of learning how to work a call from the air are two different tasks. Busy radio traffic can quickly overwhelm a new TFO and make it difficult for the trainer to evaluate how well a TFO handles a call. TFOs need to demonstrate the ability to perform each task independently before combining them. When TFOs demonstrate proficiency in both areas, then the tasks should be combined.

When less experienced TFOs realize that they are missing calls, they often try to correct the problem by increasing the volumes on all their radios. This usually makes the problem worse, because high-volume settings can make it difficult for TFOs to concentrate. It is also more fatiguing and makes it harder for them to hear what the pilot is saying on the intercom system (ICS).

If a TFO is trying to monitor all the radios at once and the trainer notices that he/she is missing calls, the trainer should have the TFO adjust the radio volumes so the radio with the lowest volume is understandable, but nothing more. The primary radio should be noticeably louder but not overwhelming. This usually enables a TFO to relax more, which is often all it takes for him/her to be able to hear the radios better.

PILOTS–MONITORING THE RADIOS

Some pilots choose not to monitor the police radios and instead listen only to the aircraft radios. There are times when this is necessary due to air traffic control (ATC) issues, but there are times when the pilot should be listening to the primary police radio. When listening to the police radio, its volume should be set lower than the volume of the aircraft's radio. The pilot's primary responsibility is safety of flight, to fly the aircraft first, and the aircraft radio is more pertinent to that than the police radio.

It is not unreasonable to expect pilots to monitor the primary police radio, but it is not surprising when they miss a call. If they are talking to a controller or to the pilot of another aircraft, for example, they are probably not going to hear what was just broadcast on the police radio. It is important for them to know what is going on so the TFO needs to keep them informed.

PATROLLING

When an aircrew is on patrol and not actively working a call, they should be flying at an altitude and airspeed that enables them to see suspicious activity on the ground. Essentially, they should use the same patrol tactics that effective ground units use. For example, officers are taught to drive slower while on patrol, because they are more likely to notice suspicious activity than when driving faster. Driving faster requires a person to pay more attention to their driving, which means they have less time to look around at their environment.

Air support units are just that–support units, and the job of the aircrew is to support officers on the ground, not find additional work for them. Sometimes, however, an aircrew will see something suspicious and they will need the assistance of ground units. Aircrews should exercise good judgment when doing this. If an aircrew is constantly generating work for other officers, those officers will be less likely to assist the aircrew on calls that they feel are less important. This does not mean that an aircrew should ignore criminal activity; it simply means that they should use discretion when requesting the assistance of ground units. No officer likes to get burdened with someone else's paperwork.

When an aircrew is on patrol, a good flight profile to use is to fly at about 60 knots at an altitude of approximately 1000 to 1200 feet AGL. At this speed and altitude, the aircrew will have adequate time to look behind businesses, at rooftops, into alleys, etc. and the helicopter will be well outside of its HV curve. At these altitudes, the aircraft generates less noise for people on the ground and the aircrew has more time to deal with emergencies. If a pilot patrols at 100 knots, noise generated by the wind can be fatiguing over time, and it will be more difficult for the aircrew to hear their radios.

TACTICALLY RESPONDING TO CALLS

Beyond the different philosophies of how aircrews respond to calls are the mechanics of actually responding. An important thing to remember is that the aircrew should not wait until they are overhead before they start working a call. An aircrew has a tremendous tactical

Figure 7. TFOs should use binoculars to look ahead at the tactical environment before they actually get to the call. They can often see suspects before the suspects can hear the helicopter.

advantage, because they can usually see the tactical environment and surrounding area before they arrive at a call. They should exploit that advantage by using their tactical equipment to look ahead at the scene when they are one or two miles out. For example, if an aircrew was responding to a vehicle burglary in progress at a shopping mall, the TFO should use binoculars to look at the scene from as far away as possible. In Figure 7, the arrow is pointing to a small shopping mall, which is about one and one half miles ahead of the aircraft. At this distance, a TFO should be able to see people in the parking lot while using binoculars. If the TFO waits until the aircraft is closer (Figure 8), the suspects will be able to hear the helicopter approaching and they will probably run before the TFO sees them.

The pilot's tactical goal when responding to calls is to fly the most direct route possible to minimize response time. There is a tendency to follow roads, especially for new pilots, because they are less familiar with the area as it looks from the air and more familiar with the streets.

Figure 8. If the aircrew waits until the aircraft is too close to the tactical environment before they start working the call, the suspects may hear the helicopter approaching and run before the TFO sees them.

When orbiting a call, the aircrew's attention is usually focused close in to the aircraft, between houses and other structures. When en route to a call, however, they need to focus their attention into the distance to determine where the call is, and then fly the most direct route. Moving maps make this task easier, but it is not unusual for the pilot to drift off course when using them.

A good method of flying the most direct route is to pick out a landmark in the distance, directly beyond where the call is located and then fly toward it. If the aircraft is equipped with a moving map, the pilot should use it to establish the aircraft's initial heading. Both crewmembers should glance down at the map occasionally to ensure that they are staying on course. If the aircraft is not equipped with a moving map, both crewmembers need to keep looking at where they think the call is located to ensure that they are headed in the right direction. It is normal to pick out new landmarks in the distance and make minor course corrections as the aircraft gets closer.

The TFO's duties while en route to a call are to assist the pilot in avoiding hazards and to ensure that the pilot is flying in the right direction. The TFO also needs to monitor the radios as information is being updated and ensure that the aircraft's tactical equipment is ready to use.

Some aircrews work in the same environment all the time and they are very familiar with the streets and landmarks. They often do not need a moving map to assist them in navigating to a call. Occasionally, however, they will get dispatched to a call and they think they know where it is, but they are wrong. Good crew coordination habits and practices will minimize the likelihood of making these mistakes. If the aircraft is equipped with a moving map, the TFO should type in the address of the call, even if the aircrew is sure that they know where it is. This is an effective method of confirming its location and it also enables the TFO to look at the names of the surrounding streets in the area in case a suspect runs after they arrive.

The TFO should also be getting pertinent information about the call while en route. The descriptions of suspects and their vehicles are important, even if the call is taking place indoors, and even if there is no indication that the suspect is leaving. It often takes several minutes for a call to be updated, and in that time a suspect might leave on foot or in a vehicle. If the aircrew knows what the suspect is wearing, or knows what kind of vehicle the suspect has, they might see the suspect leaving. If the aircrew waits until they are overhead before getting that information, they might fly right past the suspect and never know it.

RESPONDING TO CALLS QUICKLY

When an aircrew gets dispatched to a call they should not delay their response unless there is a good, legitimate reason to. If they have a choice of flying to a call at 60 knots or 100 knots they should fly at 100 knots. This does not mean the aircraft should be flown at the ragged edge of its limitations, but the aircrew should not waste time getting to a call.

Sometimes there are legitimate reasons to surveil a call from a distance and not go directly to the scene. When responding to certain crimes in progress, for example, it might be more productive for the aircrew to climb to a higher altitude and surveil the scene from a distance with binoculars before ground units arrive. When a call is taking place inside, however, the aircrew should fly directly to the scene without delay.

It is not unusual for radio calls to turn out to be something completely different than what was originally dispatched, and "routine" calls sometimes turn into major incidents. By getting to a scene quickly the aircrew can often tell the responding ground units what they are up against and provide them with important information. They might see a suspect leave or conceal evidence somewhere, or they might be able to tell officers that they are no longer needed.

DAYTIME ORBIT PROFILES

When arriving at nonurgent calls in the daytime, the pilot should position the aircraft so both crewmembers can see the tactical environment outside. This means that if the pilot is flying from the right seat, the aircraft should be positioned so the tactical environment is on the left side of the aircraft, and vice versa for pilots who fly from the left seat. The pilot should consider safety, noise, and the aircrew's ability to see details on the ground when determining where to position the aircraft.

A good orbit profile to use when orbiting nonurgent calls is to fly at approximately 50 knots, at about 800 feet above ground level (AGL), with a lateral offset of about the length of two city blocks. The size of city blocks can differ somewhat from city to city, but these are good references with which aircrews should become familiar. This orbit profile enables the pilot and TFO to see the perimeter of a residence, for example, or to keep an eye on an officer during a traffic stop or field interview. Oftentimes, there are legitimate reasons to fly lower, but absent those reasons, aircrews should fly higher for safety and noise considerations.

The ability of an aircrew to see details on the ground with the naked eye depends on their distance from the scene and their visual acuity. The straight-line distance between the aircraft and the tactical environment is called the hypotenuse distance between two points. Aircrews do not need to know what that is, but it is helpful to have a target altitude and offset in mind when orbiting a call.

The aircrew's viewing angle of an incident will remain the same if altitude and lateral offset are changed proportionately. For example, an aircrew's perspective of a call will be the same at 1000 feet AGL with a two block lateral offset as it will at 750 feet AGL with a one and

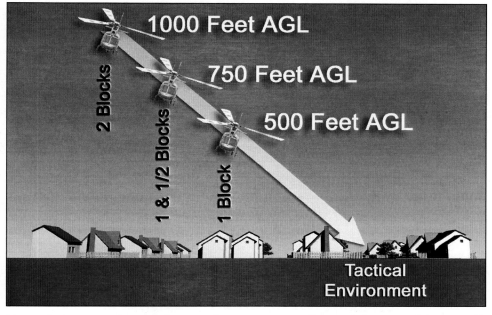

Figure 9. An aircrew's view of a tactical environment will remain the same if the aircraft's altitude and lateral offset are changed proportionately.

one half block lateral offset. It will also be the same if they descend to 500 feet AGL and reduce the aircraft's lateral offset to one block (Figure 9).

Airspeed is important, because in coordinated flight, airspeed affects the aircraft's angle of bank, and the aircraft's angle of bank affects how well the pilot can see the tactical environment outside the aircraft. When looking outside, the pilot will be looking past the TFO and there are some things in the cockpit that can obstruct their view. For example, how high the pilot sits in the seat, the physical size of the TFO, how the TFO holds his hand controllers, how he wears his kneeboard, and how he sits all affect the pilot's ability to see outside.

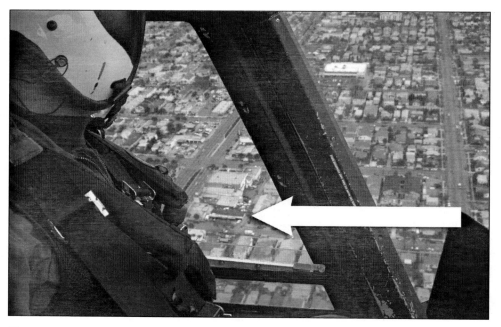

Figure 10. The arrow is pointing to a building, and the aircrew is watching the perimeter of that building. In the daytime, pilots should position the helicopter so both crewmembers have a good view of the tactical environment outside the aircraft.

Figure 10 is a picture taken from the pilot's seat during an orbit. The arrow is pointing to the tactical environment and the aircraft is flying at 800 feet AGL with a lateral offset of about two blocks. The airspeed is approximately 50 knots, which provides a sufficient angle of bank for the pilot to see past the TFO. Should an officer at the scene get into a foot pursuit or have a physical confrontation with a suspect, both crewmembers should be able to see it from this orbit profile.

In Figure 10, the TFO is wearing a survival vest, which limits the pilot's view of the tactical environment. It is easy to see how the pilot could lose sight of something if the aircraft rolled or yawed to the right. When looking outside, the pilot usually has to lean forward slightly and look 90 degrees to the left to keep the aircraft positioned effectively. If the pilot was flying from the left seat, this would be reversed. Pilots should always keep in mind that when they are looking 90 degrees to the left or right, it is more difficult to see things that are in front of the aircraft.

There are times when the pilot will not be able to spend much time looking at the tactical environment. When flying near other aircraft, near towers, or highrise buildings, for example, the pilot will often have to rely on information from the TFO to position the aircraft. In those cases, good crew coordination skills are necessary.

Another thing to consider is the time it takes to complete a single orbit. If airspeed remains constant, it will take twice as long to complete an orbit with a two block lateral offset than it will with a one block lateral offset. Therefore, if the aircrew thinks that a suspect might try to escape from the perimeter of a building, the pilot should fly faster and/or closer to the tactical environment. This will reduce the time it takes to orbit the building, which will minimize the time a suspect has to escape.

Some pilots fly the exact same orbit profile on all types of calls. Aircrews should experiment with different orbit profiles to see what works best during different scenarios. A good practice for pilots is to think about what would happen at any given time if the engine quit. Pilots do not need to be paranoid about this, because aircraft engines are extremely reliable, but if a mission could be flown effectively from a higher altitude, the pilot should fly higher.

Flying higher also enables the aircraft to accelerate quickly, if necessary. This is helpful when the aircrew is covering on a low priority call and they hear a higher priority call get dispatched elsewhere. The pilot can accelerate quickly by descending, trading altitude for airspeed. This may only shave off a few seconds from their response time, but in the airborne law enforcement business, seconds count.

When working a call, the pilot should not hover unless there is a reason to, and only then if it is safe to do so. It is usually more effective for the aircrew to orbit and surveil the overall perimeter. Sometimes the TFO needs to look in between two narrowly spaced walls with binoculars, and hovering for a moment makes this easier to do. When hovering, however, the aircraft loses its angle of bank, which causes the lower side of the aircraft on the inside of the orbit to rise. This may cause the pilot to lose sight of the tactical environment behind the airframe. In those situations, the TFO will likely have to give the pilot directions on how to position the aircraft.

WATCHING PERIMETERS IN THE DAYTIME

If officers are inside a house and the aircrew does not see anything suspicious outside, they should continue to watch the tactical environment until the ground units say they no longer need air support. Someone might try to escape from a backdoor or from a window and the officers inside the house might not know it. If the aircrew hears a more urgent call get dispatched elsewhere, they should not leave without checking in with the ground units. The aircrew has no way of knowing what is going on inside the house. Some calls may be so urgent that the aircrew must leave, but they should at least tell the ground units that they are leaving.

If officers are standing outside a house, the aircrew should remain overhead until the officers say they no longer need air support. How important is this when there is no indication of trouble? It is important because the aircrew can see things that the ground units cannot.

In 1981, two San Diego Police Officers were murdered when they were ambushed in front of a house. They were investigating a disturbance between two neighbors and the suspect came out from the rear of his house. He snuck up behind the officers and shot them, and the officers never knew he was there. There had been no indication that the suspect would attack the officers, nor was there any way for the officers to see the suspect approaching them. The San Diego Police Department did not have air support in 1981, but this is a good example of what an aircrew could be looking for, and perhaps prevent, even if the call does not initially seem to be urgent.

RESPONDING TO CRIMES IN PROGRESS

There are different methods of responding to crimes in progress and each call needs to be evaluated individually. In this actual example, it was daytime and a witness called the police to report a Hispanic male breaking into a car behind a business, which was located mid-block in a strip mall. The aircrew's ETA was three minutes and the nearest ground unit was five minutes out. The dispatcher tried to get more information, but the witness hung up.

Since they only had a vague description of the suspect, how should the aircrew have handled the call? Should they have delayed their response to coincide with that of the ground units? Should they have surveilled the scene from a distance with binoculars before ground units arrived, or should they have gone directly to the scene?

There is no absolute right or wrong answer, because all scenarios are going to be different, but aircrews should always make the best use of their tactics and equipment. In this scenario, the aircrew decided to surveil the scene with binoculars from an inconspicuous distance and look for suspicious activity. The address indicated that the call was mid-block so the TFO knew generally where to look. Within moments, the TFO saw a Hispanic male walking away quickly from an area where several cars were parked. It did not appear that the suspect knew the helicopter was there, because it was more than a mile away. The TFO relayed what they saw to the responding officers and they all converged on the suspect at the same time. The suspect ran as soon as he heard the helicopter but was quickly apprehended by ground units. He had stolen a car radio.

It is impossible to know what the suspect would have done if the aircrew had flown directly to the scene, but by holding off and surveilling the scene from a distance, the aircrew was able to identify a possible suspect and coordinate everyone's response.

When surveilling a suspect from a distance, the TFO will likely have to tell the pilot how to position the aircraft, because the pilot will not be able to see what the TFO can see. That is okay and is, in fact, desirable. If the aircraft is close enough for the pilot to clearly see the suspect with the naked eye, it is probably too close and the suspect may become suspicious of the helicopter.

The aircrew should judge their distance from a suspect by carefully balancing three factors: (1) the time it will take to fly to the scene; (2)

a distance that will not alarm the suspect; (3) a distance that is close enough for the TFO to see with binoculars. If the TFO is using ten-power binoculars, for example, a good approximate distance is about one and one-half miles, at an altitude of approximately 1500 feet AGL, depending on obstructions.

Sometimes it is more effective to climb to an altitude of several thousand feet and surveil a suspect from a more vertical angle. Suspects are usually not suspicious of helicopters at these altitudes. If the aircraft is equipped with a powerful camera system, both crewmembers will be able to see the suspect on the display. If the TFO is using binoculars, the pilot probably will not be able to see the suspect. If the pilot pays attention to where the TFO is looking, however, it is fairly easy to maneuver the aircraft effectively. As the aircraft maneuvers, the pilot should make sure that the aircraft's shadow does not pass over the suspect.

When surveilling suspects from a distance, good crew communication skills are important. If the TFO sees a suspect, for example, but the pilot is not familiar with the area, the TFO should describe landmarks near the suspect that the pilot can see. In all likelihood, the suspect is going to start running when the helicopter or ground units get close, so the pilot needs to know exactly where to go when it is time to move in.

Another thing to consider is the direction the aircraft is facing. Suspects might be able to see the helicopter in the distance, but if it is far enough away and not facing toward them, they might think the aircrew is doing something else.

In addition to employing good crew coordination skills, the TFO needs to communicate effectively with the ground units. Those officers need to have a clear understanding of what they are supposed to do, the suspect's description and location, and how to approach the area without being seen. Everyone needs to be aware that there may be more than one suspect and one of them might be acting as a lookout.

The TFO should not come off the binoculars unless it is necessary. Binoculars have a relatively narrow field of view, however, which will make it more difficult for the TFO to see ground units moving into the area. The pilot often has a better overall view and will probably be able to see the marked patrol cars before the TFO can. The pilot can often provide the TFO with staging locations for ground units to ensure that they do not compromise the surveillance. Workload permitting, the pilot may even be able to talk directly to the ground units without having to relay through the TFO. Relaying detailed information through the TFO takes time and sometimes there is not enough time to get the information out quickly. It is also less confusing if the person with detailed information can speak directly to the ground units.

When everyone is in position and it is time to move in, the TFO should keep watching the suspect(s) with the binoculars. The pilot should fly to the scene as fast as possible, because suspects will usually run when they see or hear the helicopter approaching. When the helicopter is close enough for the TFO to be able to see the suspect(s) without binoculars, he/she should make a mental note of landmarks near the suspect and then make a quick transition from the binoculars to the naked eye.

If the TFO sees a crime occurring before ground units arrive, what should the aircrew do? Should they descend on the suspect and risk initiating a foot chase with no ground units nearby or should they continue to surveil the suspect from a distance? If a suspect is committing a violent crime, the aircrew should go to the scene immediately. The aircraft's presence is often enough to make suspects stop what they are doing. If a suspect is breaking into a car or committing a similar non-violent property crime, however, the aircrew should strongly consider surveilling the suspect from a distance. This will provide officers with more time to get into the area, which will increase the likelihood of apprehending the suspect.

The reality is, the suspect has committed these crimes in the past and will continue to commit them until arrested. Moving in prematurely and preventing this particular crime will have little or no impact on preventing the suspect from committing them in the future. Arresting the suspect, however, will have an immediate impact.

What if the TFO does not see anything while searching with binoculars? Should the aircrew remain clear of the area until after the ground units arrive or should they fly directly to the scene? They should fly to the scene, because waiting for ground units to arrive surrenders the important tactical advantage of being able to get to a scene quickly. If the ground units get there first and the suspect runs, the aircrew may not be positioned effectively to assist in a foot pursuit. If the aircrew arrives first they can conduct a more thorough search before ground units arrive. They might find the suspect hiding somewhere that was not visible to them from a distance. If the suspect starts running as the aircraft approaches, the ground units should be only moments away. If the aircrew does not see anything suspicious, they should watch the area until officers arrive. Those officers might find the suspect hiding somewhere that was not visible to the aircrew.

The aircrew needs to remember that their response time from a distance of one mile is going to be about forty-five seconds if the aircraft is capable of flying at 120 mph, because the aircraft has to accelerate. A healthy suspect could probably run a block in that time so it is important for the TFO to coordinate everyone's response.

CRIMES THAT HAVE JUST OCCURRED

There is a distinct difference between crimes in progress and crimes that have just occurred, and the information the aircrew gets while en route should determine how they respond. In this example, two suspects committed a theft and then drove northbound in a blue pickup five minutes prior to the victim calling the police. The aircrew was responding from the north with a five minute ETA.

In most cases, the pilot should be able to help the TFO look for the suspects. If they have to fly through congested airspace with multiple control towers, however, the pilot may be of limited help. In congested airspace, the TFO should not assume that the pilot is hearing updates on the police radio. When practical, he/she should provide the pilot with updated information as it becomes available. An updated vehicle description or a different direction of travel is important, because the pilot may have to make course changes which will require a modified clearance through the airspace.

The TFO should be helping the pilot avoid hazards while en route to a call but the aircrew needs to get more information about the call. What kind of information would be helpful? Pickups come in all shapes and sizes with many different accessories. In large cities, the aircrew may fly over dozens of blue pickups, but in rural areas, they might not see any. To maximize their chances of spotting the suspect's vehicle, it would be helpful to have additional information. For example, what shade of blue is the truck and does it have a shell? If so, what color is it? If not, is there a tool box in the bed? Is the truck raised with oversize tires and chrome rims? Is it a full size truck or a small truck? Does it have an extended cab or four doors, or does it have any noticeable damage or primer spots? At night, it is nice to know if all of the vehicle's lights are working, because inoperative headlights are fairly noticeable.

Most people do not realize how difficult it can be for aircrews to determine the color of some vehicles at night. The red-tinted street lights found in many cities, in combination with the aircraft's distance from the vehicle, can make it difficult to identify colors.

The aircrew's ETA, the time delay, and traffic conditions are also important factors. If the call is relatively fresh, within the past five minutes or so, and the aircraft is only two or three minutes out, the suspects will only be able to travel just so far. If traffic conditions are heavy, the suspects may be stuck in traffic or at a traffic light. Do they have immediate access to freeways? What are the races of the suspects? That might be important, because if their races do not match the predominant racial makeup of the area where the crime occurred, the aircrew might be able to predict some likely escape routes. The TFO should not monopolize the radio and ask all of these questions when en route to every call, but it is a good idea to let dispatchers know how helpful this information is.

Should an aircrew respond directly to a scene or should they search the area? That depends on the type of call and the information they get while en route. In the previous example, they will likely be less effective if they respond directly to the scene. The information they have is that the suspects have been gone for five minutes and the aircrew has a five-minute response time. It is entirely possible that the suspects might return or they might be parked a block away, but in all likelihood, they are not waiting around for the police. In this example, the TFO should be getting as much information as possible while en route in order to estimate how far the suspects could drive in ten minutes.

The aircrew should check the likely escape routes, because if they fly directly to the scene and start working outward, the suspects will have progressively more time to get out of the area. Other officers are responding to the scene and they will tell the aircrew if they are needed there.

Many times, suspects flee crime scenes by driving out of the area on less-traveled residential streets. The fastest routes into and out of an area are usually the main streets and suspects will often avoid those routes to avoid being seen. The aircrew has the unique advantage of being able to see several different escape routes simultaneously so they should not focus their attention only on the main streets.

How does an aircrew determine if a vehicle leaving the area is the suspect's vehicle? In many cases, victims and witnesses do not have a lot of information. The aircrew may only know that the suspects left in a dark sedan. This is when the aircrew needs to rely on their law enforcement experience and pay close attention to what they see. Sometimes it is the smallest of details that arouse suspicion. Is the vehicle a dark sedan? If not, could it be mistaken for one? Remember, colors can be hard to identify at night, even for people on the ground. Is the car moving quickly out of the area and not stopping at intersections, or does the driver pull over and stop for no apparent reason? If no one gets out of the car, the occupants may be looking up at the helicopter to see if it is following them. Many suspects know that a moving vehicle attracts more attention than a parked vehicle.

Does it look like the driver is familiar with the area or are they driving around as if trying to find a way out of the area? Some suspects have their windows rolled down and their sunroofs open to listen for the helicopter. If so, the aircrew might be able to see the occupants. Do they match the descriptions of the suspects? Are they looking up at the helicopter as if to see if it is following them or do they seem disinterested? Is their vehicle the only one in the area with its windows down and sunroof open, and is that unusual for the weather conditions?

READING LICENSE PLATES

It is helpful when a witness gets the license plate of a suspect's vehicle, but it can be very difficult to read license plates from a helicopter, even with stabilized binoculars. Reading license plates is not always an unsafe practice, but it often involves increased risk, because the pilot will likely have to descend and fly slower to enable the TFO to read the plate.

Several factors need to be considered before the TFO tries to read a license plate. For example, is the vehicle on an open road with no obstructions going 65 mph or is it downtown between some highrise buildings moving slowly? Clearly, the first scenario involves less risk than the second. Are the suspects parolees wanted for armed robbery or are they teenagers who stole some beer? Are there any officers nearby who could read the license plate or is the aircrew the only law enforcement presence in the area?

Sometimes the pilot may have to hover or fly sideways so the TFO can read the license plate out a side window. Pilots have to be extremely careful when doing this, especially when the aircraft is heavy or when it is moving downwind. The helicopter is going to have a tendency to weather-vane and the pilot may not have enough tail rotor authority to overcome it. If the pilot encounters a loss of tail rotor effectiveness, the aircraft may start spinning. If that occurs, the only way to recover may be to lower the collective and generate forward airspeed. When the pilot lowers the collective, the aircraft is going to descend. If the pilot was already flying low to enable the TFO to read the license plate, there may not be enough altitude to recover. If the pilot tries to recover by pulling up on the collective, the main rotor RPM may droop and the tail rotor will become even less effective. This will exacerbate the problem and will likely cause significant damage to the helicopter's drive train components, even if the pilot is able to recover. It is usually a better idea to direct ground units to a vehicle and let them read the license plate.

What should the aircrew do with license plate information? Should they fly directly to the registered owner's house? Not necessarily, but they might want to fly the most likely routes between the crime scene and the house and then surveil it from an inconspicuous distance. If the suspects are headed home, they are probably going to see the helicopter if it is orbiting over their house at 500 feet and they may not go home. If the aircrew decides to surveil the house, they should do so from a distance of no less than one and one-half miles, at an altitude that gives the TFO a clear view of the house and the likely approach routes. The suspects might still be able to see the helicopter, but if it is far enough away, they might think that the aircrew is doing something else.

RESPONDING TO URGENT CALLS

One of the most common complaints about helicopters is their noise, but sometimes that noise can be useful, because it has a deterring effect on suspects and a reassuring effect on officers on the ground. When responding to urgent calls for cover, for example, the aircrew should take advantage of the aircraft's noise and arrive faster and lower than they normally would–but not excessively. This tactic gets the attention of officers and suspects. They know that help has arrived and more is coming. That may be all it takes to convince a suspect to stop fighting. The effect is usually achieved within the first two orbits so the aircraft should not remain at a lower altitude any longer than necessary. The pilot needs to maintain good forward airspeed to avoid a loss of tail rotor effectiveness, especially when turning downwind. The aircrew's attention is going to be focused 90 degrees to the left or right, so they need to be aware of any nearby hazards, especially at night. When responding to urgent calls in this manner, there is rarely a reason to descend any lower than 300 feet AGL. The risks associated with flying lower can be significant.

Chapter 3

COVERING OFFICERS ON THE STREET

When officers are conducting field interviews with suspects on the street, or when they are conducting traffic stops with no cover, the aircrew can cover them by orbiting at an altitude that lets the suspects know the helicopter is there. The aircrew cannot hear what is being said, but that does not mean that they are not being effective. Essentially, the aircrew is trying to intimidate the suspect–not overtly, but just enough to let them know that they are being watched. The aircraft should not make any more noise than is necessary, because it might be difficult for the officer to communicate with the suspect.

A good orbit profile to use when covering officers in nonurgent situations is to fly at approximately 50 knots, at about 800 feet AGL, with a lateral offset of about the length of two city blocks. At this altitude, experienced TFOs can often see a suspect's body language, which may indicate that he is about to run or fight. If there is a reason to believe that a suspect might flee or become violent, the pilot should descend to approximately 500 feet AGL with a lateral offset of about one block. The TFO should not hesitate to request additional cover if the officer has not already done so. When cover units arrive, the pilot should climb to a higher altitude when it becomes apparent that the situation is under control. The aircrew should remain overhead until the ground units say air support is no longer needed.

When covering officers on the street, there are some things that TFOs can do to prepare themselves for a foot pursuit, even if there is no indication that the suspect is going to run. For example, the TFO should consciously be thinking about directions (north, south, east, and west). It is surprising how often TFOs broadcast the wrong direction of travel during a foot pursuit, even when they are familiar with the area. The stress of a foot pursuit can quickly overload a TFO if he/she is not mentally prepared for it. TFOs should also be noting the suspect's description. They should pay particular attention to any secondary layers of clothing that might be visible under the suspect's jacket or shirt. When suspects run, they often try to change their appearance by taking off an outer layer of clothing. If the TFO waits until the suspect runs before noting their description, there might not be enough time to get it.

Suspects obviously know when the helicopter is overhead. When they run, they will try to outrun the ground units and hide from the aircrew. Therefore, the TFO should also be thinking about the names of the streets in the area. It is going to be more difficult to remember them during the stress of a foot pursuit, and there will not be enough time to bring up the moving map or read from a map book.

ALTERNATIVE ORBIT PROFILES

Suspects know that if they cannot see the helicopter, the aircrew cannot see them. If suspects are going to become violent or run, they are more likely to do so when the helicopter is out of sight.

Figure 11 is an overhead view of a daytime traffic stop and the arrow is pointing to the officer. Figure 12 is a side view of the same location. These two diagrams represent what an orbit profile should look like when there are no obstructions between the aircrew and the officer. The orbit profile should be a fairly concentric circle. Unless there is a reason to believe that the suspect might become violent or run, the pilot should be orbiting at approximately 50 knots, at an altitude of about 800 feet AGL with a lateral offset of about the length of two city blocks. This orbit profile will enable both crew members to have a good view of the tactical environment.

In low-wind conditions, the aircrew's view of the tactical environment will move horizontally and vertically slightly, as the pilot corrects for wind, but it should not be difficult for both crew members to keep the tactical environment in sight. The airspeed should remain fairly constant and in low-wind conditions, the ground speed will vary only slightly. As the wind becomes stronger, the pilot should ensure that the aircraft does not lose translational lift when moving down-

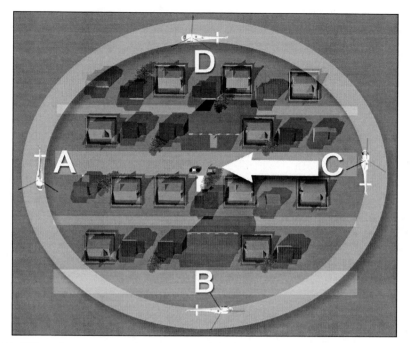

Figure 11. When there are no obstructions to block the aircrew's view, a concentric orbit should be flown around officers when the aircrew is providing them with cover.

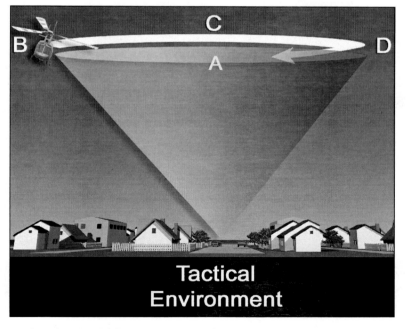

Figure 12. The pilot should fly a concentric orbit around the tactical environment, unless obstructions prevent them from doing so.

wind, and the pilot should try to maintain a relatively constant ground speed and distance from the scene. This gives the TFO the best overall view of the tactical environment on all sides of the orbit.

ORBITING TALL STRUCTURES

When an officer and suspect are standing next to a building, it will be impossible for the aircrew to keep them in sight if the pilot flies a normal orbit profile (Figure 13). When the aircraft is on the back side of the structure, the officer and suspect will be out of sight for an uncomfortable period of time (Figure 14). In those situations, the pilot can either hover, or modify the aircraft's orbit profile to keep the officer and suspect in sight.

Figure 15 is an overhead view of where an officer and suspect are standing near the base of a two-story apartment building. Figure 16 is a side view of that same location. These two diagrams represent what an orbit profile should look like when the aircrew's view is blocked by

Figure 13. The arrow is pointing to an officer who is standing next to an apartment building. The aircrew can only see the officer on the front side of the orbit.

obstructions. The aircraft should be flown at approximately 800 feet AGL, but the orbit profile should be more of an oval racetrack pattern than a concentric circle, and the aircraft's orbit should be offset from the tactical environment.

Figure 14. The arrow is pointing to an officer on the far side of an apartment building. When the aircraft is on the backside of the orbit, the officer and suspect will not be visible for an uncomfortable period of time.

When the helicopter is in Position D it should be very close to the tactical environment. The pilot should be flying faster in Position D and increase the aircraft's angle of bank. This will enable the TFO to see over the edge of the building better. Flying faster in this part of the orbit also minimizes the time spent in this region of less visibility. As the helicopter passes Position D, the pilot should skid the tail of the aircraft slightly to the right to ensure that the TFO can see the officer and suspect. The aircraft will be out of rig for a moment and the pilot may momentarily lose sight of the officer and suspect, but the TFO should still be able to see them. As the aircraft approaches Position A, the pilot should slow down and decrease the aircraft's angle of bank. The

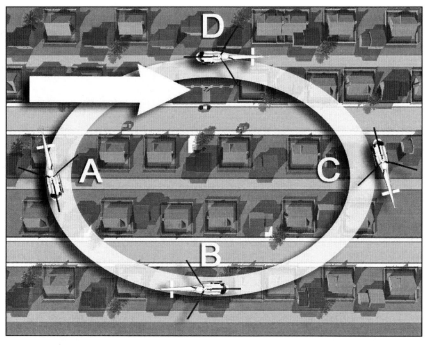

Figure 15. The arrow is pointing to an officer and a suspect who are standing next to a tall building. The aircraft's orbit profile and airspeed should be modified so the aircrew can keep the officer and suspect in sight.

airspeed should be slower than normal throughout the rest of the orbit but not so slow as to lose translational lift. Flying slower in Positions A, B, and C will enable the pilot and TFO to spend more time watching the officer and suspect. When the helicopter passes Position C, the pilot should accelerate again and repeat the orbit.

An alternative is to hover in a spot that enables the aircrew to see the officer and suspect at all times, but this should only be done if it can be done safely. When working near downtown highrise buildings, hovering or flying very slow may be necessary. Some highrise buildings are so high and so close together that the TFO will not have much time to search for someone or cover an officer effectively. Hovering may be the only way to keep them in sight.

The problems associated with working in downtown highrise environments are amplified by the fact that there are often a large number of people present. Searching for suspects in those environments can be very difficult.

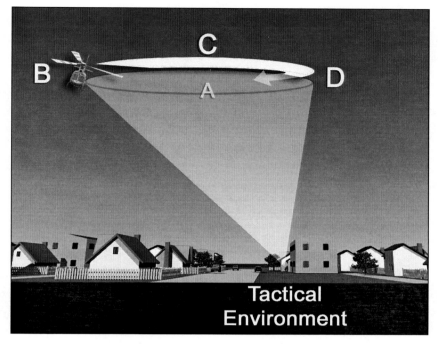

Figure 16: When an officer and suspect are standing next to a tall structure, the aircraft's orbit profile should not be a concentric circle. The orbit should be shifted off-center, and the airspeed should be modified.

DAYTIME, HIGH-RISK TRAFFIC STOPS

When covering officers on high-risk traffic stops in the daytime, the aircrew must remember that the ground units will need to communicate with the suspects in the vehicle. Those officers are going to be telling the suspects exactly what to do, and if the suspects do not comply, their lack of compliance might be interpreted as aggression. Absent a reason to fly lower, the pilot should fly high enough to ensure that the aircraft's noise does not interfere with the officers' ability to communicate with the suspects.

Aircrews must pay close attention to what suspects do during high-risk vehicle stops. The aircraft should not be flown any lower than is necessary, but the aircrew must be prepared for a foot pursuit (Chapter 8). When a vehicle pursuit terminates, it is very common for the driver to flee on foot. In those scenarios, the aircrew should remain at an altitude that enables them to maintain visual contact with the suspect. If there are multiple suspects, some of them may remain in the vehicle, and there is no way for anyone to know if those suspects are armed or what their intentions are.

If suspects are going to flee from a vehicle during a high-risk traffic stop, they are probably going to do it immediately after the vehicle stops. Suspects know that they have a better chance of escaping if they flee before additional officers arrive. There is no guarantee that they will not run at a later time, but it is not as common.

If no one flees from the vehicle, the pilot should fly high enough to ensure that the aircraft's noise does not interfere with the ability of the officers to communicate with the suspects. Once again, a good orbit profile to use is to fly at approximately 50 knots, at about 800 feet AGL, with a lateral offset of about two blocks. Some aircraft are quieter than others, so aircrews should experiment to see what orbit profile works best for them and their ground units.

When the last known suspect has exited the vehicle, ground units sometimes ask the aircrew to look inside it to see if anyone is hiding. To do this, the pilot is probably going to have to descend and fly slower or hover. Risk management must play a role in the aircrew's decision on whether or not to do this. If the crime involved a rifle, for example, the last thing the pilot should do is descend and/or hover. Other things to consider are the wind's direction and speed, the environment beneath the aircraft and available power. It is not unreasonable for ground units to make this request, but the aircrew must consider the risks before doing it.

It is frequently impossible for a TFO to say with 100 percent certainty that there is no one else in the vehicle. In the daytime, glare on the vehicle's windows, or tinted windows will make it difficult for the TFO to see inside. If someone is hiding in the vehicle, it is possible that a TFO will not be able to see them. There is nothing wrong with looking, if reasonable precautions are taken, but a TFO should never leave ground units with the impression that there is no one else in a vehicle.

NIGHTTIME, HIGH-RISK TRAFFIC STOPS

When high-risk traffic stops are conducted at night, the same general rules apply to chasing suspects who run from the vehicle. Some high-risk stops, however, are conducted in relatively well-lit areas, while others are conducted in very dark environments. If a suspect stops in a well-lit area and does not immediately run, the aircraft should remain in a high orbit profile to minimize noise. In well-lit areas, the searchlight should not be used unless ground units request it, and the TFO should be watching the vehicle with the FLIR.

If a suspect stops in a very dark environment, the aircrew should immediately become suspicious, especially if it looks like the suspect intentionally sought out a dark area to stop. It is entirely possible that the suspect stopped there because it was convenient, but it is also possible, and reasonable, to assume that the suspect intends to use the darkness to his advantage.

When covering on high-risk traffic stops in dark environments, the aircrew should orbit overhead and illuminate the suspect's vehicle with the searchlight until adequate cover arrives. The aircraft's altitude should be no lower than is necessary for the light to be effective. The aircrew must also ensure that the light does not illuminate officers on the ground, because the suspect(s) should not be allowed to know how many officers there are or where they are. The searchlight not only intimidates suspects, it also illuminates them in case officers have to shoot.

When cover units arrive, the TFO should ask the ground units if they still need the searchlight. They are the best judges of whether or not they need it, or if the aircraft's noise is interfering with their ability to communicate. Officer safety is the highest priority, and in this particular scenario, the searchlight provides the greatest officer safety benefits.

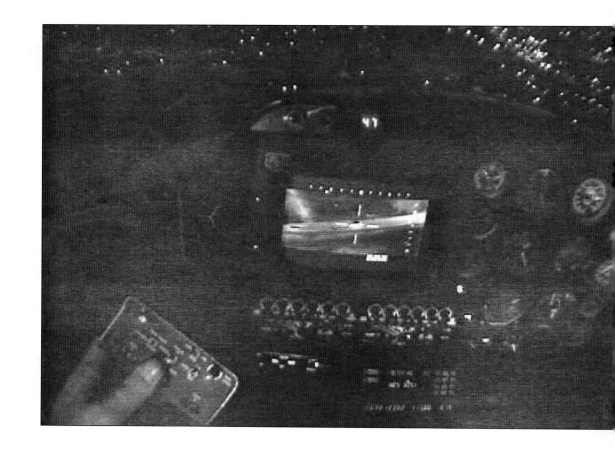

Chapter 4

FUNDAMENTALS OF THERMAL IMAGING

Many of the tactics described in this book were designed around the use of thermal imagers. Thermal imaging is the most effective method of searching for people at night under most conditions. The science of infrared spectroscopy is beyond the scope of this book, but it is helpful to have a fundamental understanding of what thermal imagers do and why they are so effective.

Thermal imagers are effective because they do not rely on reflected infrared energy. They also detect emitted infrared energy, and people often have relatively high heat emissions. Suspects usually do not think in terms of hiding their infrared emissions; they are usually more concerned about hiding their visual appearance.

When a searchlight is used to search for a suspect in a canyon, for example, the aircrew is relying on reflected visible light from the searchlight to see the contrast between the suspect and the suspect's surroundings. It is very difficult to find a suspect with a searchlight if he/she is hiding in dense brush, especially if the suspect's clothing blends in with the surroundings.

If that same suspect were to shine a flashlight up at the helicopter, however, the light from the flashlight would contrast sharply against the dark background and would be very easy to see. Essentially, this is exactly what suspects are doing with their body heat, but instead of emitting visible light, they are emitting infrared energy, which contrasts sharply with the relatively cool surroundings.

The infrared systems used by airborne law enforcement detect infrared energy in either the 3 to 5, or 8 to 12 micron frequencies. A micron is a unit of measurement, and one micron is one-millionth of a meter.

Figure 17 is a diagram of the infrared spectrum. The gray shaded areas labeled 3 to 5, and 8 to 12, are regions of high atmospheric transmission, which means infrared energy radiates well in those regions. The black shaded areas are areas of attenuation, or frequencies of infrared energy that are filtered out by the atmosphere. No airborne law enforcement thermal imagers operate in these regions.

Thermal imagers are passive, nonintrusive systems, and they do not transmit or emit any energy. They simply detect infrared energy that is radiated from the surface of various objects. A thermal imager functions very much like a video camera. It detects energy, and electronically converts that energy to a display that can be viewed. The primary difference is, video cameras are sensitive to visible light energy, and thermal imagers are sensitive to infrared energy.

Approximately 60 percent of the sun's radiated energy is in the infrared spectrum, and the visible light spectrum is relatively small in comparison (400 to 700 nanometers vs. 780 nm to 1.0 mm (780×10^{-9} m). Most people are more comfortable operating in the visible light spectrum, because that is what the human eye can see, but there is much more information available in the infrared spectrum.

All objects absorb, emit, and reflect infrared energy, but they do so at different rates and to different degrees. Water, for example, is a good absorber and emitter of infrared energy and it can also be a good reflector of infrared energy. Water, however, is a poor transmitter of infrared energy, which explains why thermal imagers cannot detect people underwater very well. A person's body heat gets absorbed by the water and does not radiate from the water's surface.

Polished aluminum is a poor absorber and emitter of infrared energy, because it reflects about 95 percent of the infrared energy that strikes it. A polished aluminum roof on a shed, for example, will appear to be relatively cold at night, because it is reflecting infrared energy from the night sky. A cedar shake roof, however, is a good absorber and emitter of infrared energy, but it is a poor reflector. This explains why cedar shake roofs and roofs of similar construction materials appear to be fairly warm at night.

TFOs not only have to learn how to interpret the FLIR image, they also need to get comfortable operating the system itself. It can be very intimidating to learn how to use a FLIR, and it takes a relatively long period of time to become proficient. TFOs need to become familiar enough with the controls to make adjustments without having to look at the controller. If the TFO has to look at the controller to find a switch, the imager will likely drift off target. When that happens, it will create a problem for the pilot, because the pilot is going to be maneuvering the aircraft by referring to the FLIR display.

ACQUIRING OBJECTS WITH FLIR

Learning how to correlate what is seen on the FLIR's display with what is seen outside the aircraft is an essential skill. It is also one of the most difficult skills for TFOs to master. FLIR displays have symbology for azimuth and elevation information. That symbology indicates where the FLIR is pointed, and becomes more useful as the aircraft gets closer to a scene. When the aircrew is en route to a call, the TFO should use the symbology to point the FLIR in the general direction of the call. Then, the TFO should look outside and find some landmarks at or near the call. The TFO should then find those landmarks on the display. This usually means that the TFO has to glance back and forth between what is seen outside the aircraft and what is seen on the display, but that is normal. This will get easier as the aircraft gets closer to the scene and as the TFO becomes more experienced.

When the TFO has acquired the tactical environment with the FLIR, they should focus their attention primarily on the FLIR from that time on. With practice, TFOs will find it easier to acquire objects in this manner.

HUMAN INFRARED CHARACTERISTICS

Searching for suspects is one of the most common missions for aircrews, and there are three things to look for when searching for people with FLIR: (1) relatively high heat emissions; (2) well-defined edges; (3) movement. TFOs should not expect to see all three characteristics in every instance; but in many cases, one or two of them will be present.

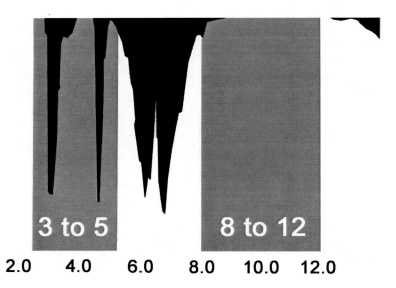

Figure 17. The gray shaded areas in this diagram are regions of high atmospheric transmission. Infrared energy radiates well in these regions. The black shaded areas are areas of attenuation, or frequencies of infrared energy that gets filtered out by the atmosphere.

Chapter 5

INFRARED SEARCHES

FLIR SEARCHES IN RESIDENTIAL AREAS

When conducting any search, the aircrew should always use the most effective search tool for any given scenario. That tool might be a FLIR, binoculars, a searchlight, night vision goggles, the naked eye, or any combination thereof.

When compared to other technology, thermal imagers are the most difficult to operate, and their use requires the highest degree of crew coordination. That is why some aircrews shy away from using them. If an aircrew can get comfortable with their equipment and tactics, however, they will be much more effective.

When an aircrew gets called to search for a suspect, they need to know the location of the call. If the aircraft is equipped with a moving map, the TFO should type in the address while en route. TFOs should familiarize themselves with the names of the streets in the area in case there is a foot pursuit after they arrive. It also helps the aircrew understand the size of the perimeter. As they approach the call, the TFO should instruct a ground unit to go to where the suspect was last seen and point their flashlight directly at the helicopter. That light will usually be visible to the aircrew when they are a mile or more away. This is an excellent method of getting the aircrew's attention so they can go directly to the scene.

The TFO then needs to know the time delay since the suspect was last seen and the suspect's last known direction of travel. The aircrew should not assume that the suspect is going to keep moving in the same direction, but it gives them a starting point to look for likely escape routes and hiding places. Once they arrive at the call, an experienced aircrew can usually tell if the perimeter needs to be modified.

When the aircraft arrives overhead, it will take a moment for the aircrew to orient themselves geographically to the tactical environment. That is normal, and it is often helpful to look outside when doing this, but the TFO should not waste time searching outside visually.

The searchlight should not initially be used to search, because at this stage, it does little more than tell the suspect where the aircrew is searching. If suspects know where the aircrew is searching, they will put more effort into hiding when the light gets near them, and they may run when it is pointed somewhere else.

If an officer is not in active foot pursuit, suspects will usually take the path of least resistance to get out of an area or they will hide. The TFO can often see the most likely escape routes with the FLIR and should not hesitate to move perimeter containment units to more effective positions. The goal is to contain the suspect in as small an area as possible as quickly as possible.

AIRCRAFT POSITIONING DURING RESIDENTIAL AREA FLIR SEARCHES

When searching for people at night, a thermal imager is far more effective than a searchlight or the human eye. There are fewer airframe obstructions around the imager, so its view of the tactical environment is better than the aircrew's view (Figures 18 & 19). Pilots should take advantage of this by positioning the helicopter closer to the tactical environment during a FLIR search. It is important to understand that "closer" does not mean "lower," it simply means that the aircraft's lateral offset distance from the tactical environment should be less than it is when searching visually in the daytime. It is often so close that the pilot will not be able to see the entire tactical environment outside the aircraft because it is too low in relation to the left side of the aircraft. That is normal.

This is when some pilots begin to encounter problems. When pilots cannot see the tactical environment outside the aircraft, they either have to watch the FLIR display to maneuver the aircraft or take commands from the TFO. The most effective option is to watch the FLIR display.

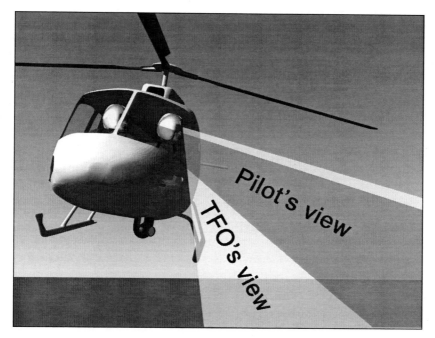

Figure 18. The TFO has a better view of the tactical environment outside the aircraft than the pilot does. The pilot's view is blocked by the airframe and other obstructions.

Figure 19. A FLIR has a better view of the tactical environment beneath the aircraft than the aircrew does. This enables the pilot to fly closer to the tactical environment when conducting a FLIR search. When the aircraft is closer, it is easier for the aircrew to see over obstructions.

Some believe that pilots should not be looking at a display when flying an aircraft, but there are a couple of points worth making to put this in perspective. First, the pilot's highest priority must always be safety of flight, i.e., to fly the aircraft first. If a pilot cannot refer to a display because it would adversely affect safety of flight, then they should not refer to it, because it is a safety issue. If safety of flight would not be adversely affected, but pilots do not refer to a display because they have not learned how, it is a training issue.

When an aircraft GPS with a moving map gets installed in an aircraft, pilots are expected to learn how and when to use it. Those displays provide the pilot with a tremendous amount of information. The same goes for multifunction displays or any other display technology. They become part of the pilot's scan when they are needed, and when it is safe and reasonable to view them. The FLIR display should be viewed with exactly the same mindset; it should be part of the pilot's scan when it is needed, and when it is safe and reasonable to view it.

Another important consideration is the pilot's field of view when orbiting a call. When the pilot is viewing the FLIR display, the aircraft's instruments, caution lights, and any obstructions that might be in front of the aircraft are easier to see peripherally than when looking outside 90 degrees to the left or right (Figures 20 & 21).

Effective aircraft positioning during a FLIR search is achieved by controlling three factors: (1) airspeed, (2) altitude, (3) lateral offset. When conducting a FLIR search in a residential area, the pilot should not be able to look past the TFO and see the entire tactical environment outside. If he/she can, the aircraft is too far away (Figure 22, Position C). The orbit profile in Position C works well in the daytime because the human eye is very efficient, and it is reasonable to believe that an aircrew might see something outside. When a suspect is hiding in a dark residential area, however, it is highly unlikely that the aircrew is going to see him when looking outside. It is too dark, there are too many obstructions for suspects to hide behind, and the aircraft's distance from those obstructions makes it impossible for the aircrew to see over them.

One might think that an ideal search angle would be 90 degrees to the tactical environment, or straight down beneath the aircraft (Figure 22, Position A). Theoretically, such an angle would allow an aircrew to see over the edge of all obstructions. In reality, however, it is very difficult to conduct a FLIR search when the imager is pointed straight

Figure 20. When both crewmembers are looking outside, 90 degrees to the left or right, hazards in front of the aircraft are more difficult to see peripherally.

Figure 21. When both crewmembers are looking at the display during a FLIR search, it is easier for them to see hazards in front of the aircraft. The display is more in line with the aircraft's direction of flight.

down. The gyros have difficulty stabilizing the gimbal, and if the aircraft has any appreciable airspeed, the image will be difficult to interpret because of its relative motion across the screen. It is also much more difficult for the aircrew to stay oriented when the imager is pointed straight down.

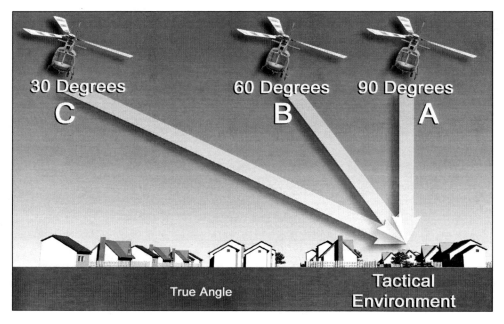

Figure 22. When an aircrew is conducting a visual search outside the aircraft, the aircraft's true angle should be approximately 30 degrees from the tactical environment (Position C). When conducting a FLIR search, however, the true angle should be approximately 60 degrees (Position B).

There are occasions, however, when the TFO might need to look straight down at something with the FLIR. When searching between two narrowly spaced walls, for example, or when trying to look down into a trash dumpster, the pilot is going to have to pay close attention to the display and maneuver the aircraft carefully. The pilot should put the object directly in front of the aircraft with the aircraft's nose facing into the wind, and then fly toward it slowly. As the aircraft gets closer it will become difficult for the TFO to keep the FLIR on target if the aircraft is moving too fast, or if the object is not directly in front of the aircraft.

When conducting a FLIR search in a residential area, the aircraft should be positioned at a true angle of about 60 degrees from the tactical environment (Figure 22, Position B). It is important to understand that the true angle is not the FLIR's gimbal angle. The true angle is the angle of the aircraft from the tactical environment when viewed from the ground. Sixty degrees can initially be somewhat difficult for an aircrew to recognize until they get used to how it looks on the display. For reference, at an altitude of 600 feet AGL, a 60 degree true angle equates to a lateral offset distance of about the length of three-quarters of a city block.

The elevation symbology on a FLIR's display is an indication of the FLIR's vertical gimbal angle in relation to the aircraft. That symbology does not indicate the aircraft's true angle from the tactical environment. If the aircraft's angle of bank and altitude remain relatively constant, however, the elevation symbology can be used to maintain a constant lateral offset distance from the tactical environment.

When the aircraft is being flown in an effective orbit profile, the elevation symbology will indicate a down-angle of approximately 35 to 40 degrees, depending on the aircraft's angle of bank. The azimuth symbology should indicate between 270 and 300 degrees to the left/front. If pilots fly from the left seat, the azimuth symbology should indicate between 60 and 90 degrees to the right/front, but the elevation symbology should be the same.

Modern infrared systems are far more capable than early generation systems, but many of the older systems are still in use. Some of the older systems have two fields of view with a zooming ability of approximately 6 to 1. Newer systems have multiple fields of view and can zoom in much closer. Tactically, the primary differences between the two generations of systems are the altitude and airspeed at which missions can be flown. During a FLIR search, the aircraft's true angle from the tactical environment should not vary between the two generations of systems. It should remain at about 60 degrees.

If the aircraft's true angle remains constant, but the aircraft's altitude is increased, the lateral offset distance from the tactical environment will also increase. If airspeed is not increased proportionately, it will take much longer to complete a single orbit. This will give a suspect more time to hide and it will take longer to complete a search. Therefore, as altitude increases, so should airspeed.

When using an older generation system, the aircraft should be flown at approximately 30 to 40 knots, at an altitude of about 600 feet AGL with a lateral offset of about three-quarters of a city block from the tactical environment. When using a newer generation system, the aircraft should be flown at approximately 50 knots, at an altitude of about 1000 feet AGL with a lateral offset of about one and one-quarter blocks. Both of these orbit profiles will provide the aircrew with a similar view of the tactical environment, because the aircraft's true angle has not changed.

These orbit profiles provide good search angles over walls and other obstructions. They also minimize noise and the time it takes to conduct a search. The helicopter can maintain translational lift, and both orbit profiles are well outside the HV curve of all helicopters.

When pilots are learning how to position the aircraft by referring to the FLIR display, their attention should be focused on maneuvering the aircraft, not on interpreting the image. That is the TFO's job. As pilots gain more experience, they will rely less on the symbology to maneuver the aircraft and more on how the image looks. Ultimately, pilots should be able to fly effective FLIR search orbits with only an occasional glance at the symbology.

SEARCH PATTERNS IN RESIDENTIAL AREAS

If the tactical environment covers half a block in a residential area, the pilot should not be orbiting the entire perimeter (unless the mission is to watch the perimeter). If the aircrew's mission is to conduct a FLIR search, the pilot should be flying smaller, concentric orbits around the immediate area that the TFO is searching (Figure 23). Essentially, this search pattern follows the same logic that ground units use when they search. Officers on the ground do not search only the front yards of houses, then return to search the backyards; they search the entire yard of a house, and then move on to the next one. That is exactly what an aircrew should do when they conduct a FLIR search.

Figure 23 is not to scale, nor is it meant to imply that only one orbit should be flown around each yard. It is simply a diagram of the pattern that should be flown when conducting a FLIR search in a residential area. In reality, the pilot may have to fly several orbits around each residence so the TFO can conduct a thorough search.

Figure 23. When an aircrew is conducting a FLIR search in a residential area, the pilot should fly multiple orbits around each house to enable the TFO to conduct a thorough search.

The aircrew should be searching two to three residences ahead of the ground units for tactical and officer-safety considerations. Tactically, suspects will not know when they have been found with the FLIR, which gives the aircrew time to get ground units into position around them. From an officer-safety perspective, a FLIR search does not expose officers to immediate threats, because they are not surprised by the suspect, nor are they in close proximity to suspects when they are found.

When conducting a FLIR search, TFOs sometimes focus all of their attention near the center of the display and not enough on the periphery. In residential areas, a FLIR's field of view will usually encompass more than one residence. If a TFO is only looking at the center of the display he/she will probably miss suspects who are hiding in neighboring yards. The best way to become proficient at spotting suspects on the periphery of the display is to become familiar with how people look on the FLIR. With experience, it will become easier for TFOs to notice objects with similar heat emissions in different areas of the display. TFOs also need to learn how to move the imager effectively during a FLIR search. It is much more difficult to notice small heat sources when the imager is moving fast or if it has jerky movements.

RESIDENTIAL AREA HIDING LOCATIONS

Suspects hide in bushes, dog houses, under boat covers, trash cans, in sheds and practically anywhere else that one could imagine. When they hide underneath or behind something, there is still a chance that the FLIR can detect their body heat. In Figure 24, heat can be seen emitting from the outer surface of a building which is made of aluminum. In this actual incident, a suspect cut a hole in the side of a building and then crawled through it. When officers searched the building, the suspect hid behind some boxes, against a wall out of their sight. He was there for about fifteen minutes and his body heat transferred through the wall and was re-emitted outside. The FLIR operator was able to detect that heat.

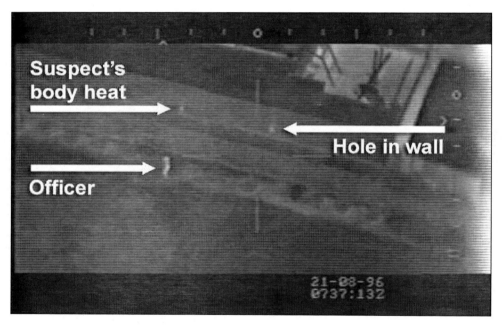

Figure 24. In this illustration, heat can be seen emitting from a building. The heat source on the right was emitting from a hole in the side of the building. The heat source on the left is the suspect's body heat that was absorbed by the metal wall, and then re-emitted outside.

That heat source could easily have been overlooked by the aircrew because it didn't look like a person. They also could have ignored it because it is not unusual for mechanical equipment to produce similar heat emissions. Fortunately, they paid attention to it as they searched the area and they noticed that it kept getting warmer. They convinced the ground units to search the building again and told them exactly where to look. The suspect was found and arrested. This incident occurred in a large structure, but the same concept applies to metal sheds, boat covers, trash cans, or any other relatively thin material. If a suspect is in physical contact with it, there is a good chance that their body heat will transfer through it.

When searching residential areas, all sides of the structures in each yard need to be scanned. This means that the pilot is going to have to position the aircraft so the TFO can see those areas. A FLIR search should be conducted in narrow field of view, but the TFO should occasionally switch to wide field of view for a moment to stay oriented. FLIR operators scan and orient themselves in wide field of view. They search, and evaluate heat sources in narrow field of view.

TFOs should only search areas that they can see. While this concept may seem obvious, less experienced TFOs often overlook it. For example, the diagrams in Figures 25 and 26 are of the same location but viewed from different angles. The arrows are pointing to where a suspect is hiding. In Figure 25, the suspect is not visible because he is lying down between two houses, and the overlapping structures are blocking the TFO's view. The aircraft's orbit profile is good, but the TFO is not taking advantage of the aircraft's position to search areas that they can see. In Figure 26, however, the TFO is taking advantage of aircraft positioning and the suspect is visible.

When suspects hide alongside houses or fences they will only be visible to the FLIR operator during certain portions of an orbit. Figure 27 is a diagram that represents a FLIR's narrow field of view. The arrow is pointing to a suspect who is lying down next to the wall of a house. The TFO is able to watch the suspect closely in narrow field of view, but the perimeters of the structures around the suspect are not visible. That is acceptable as long as the TFO can see the suspect. As the aircraft continues to orbit, however, the TFO is going to lose sight of the suspect behind the house. If the FLIR is kept in narrow field of view, neither the suspect nor the perimeters of the houses will be visible. This will give the suspect an opportunity to move around the struc-

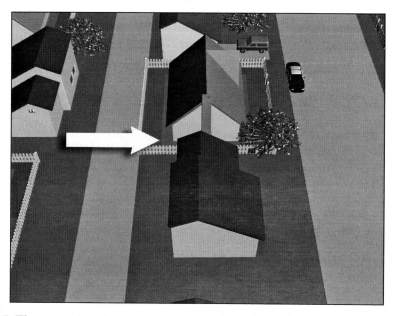

Figure 25. The arrow is pointing to a suspect, who is lying down between two houses. When conducting a FLIR search, TFOs should only search areas that they can see. When structures overlap each other, the TFO will not be able to see in between them until the aircraft is better positioned.

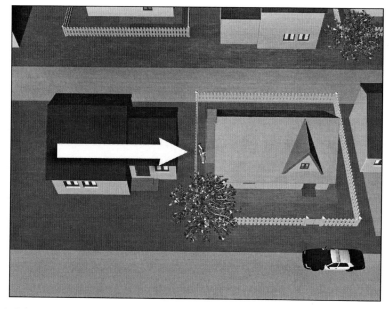

Figure 26. The arrow is pointing to a suspect who is lying down between two houses. When conducting a FLIR search, the TFO should take advantage of the aircraft's position and only search areas that they can see. At this angle, a TFO would be able to see the suspect.

tures without being seen, and they will be able to escape from an area of the perimeter that is not visible in narrow field of view. Remember, suspects know that if they cannot see the helicopter, the aircrew cannot see them.

A more effective tactic is to switch to wide field of view immediately after losing sight of the suspect in narrow field of view (Figure 28). Even though the suspect is not visible behind the house, the perimeters of the houses are visible, so the suspect will not be able to escape without being seen. This FLIR tactic applies to all situations when an object is no longer visible in narrow field of view. Switching to wide field of view is the fastest way to reacquire it, and it is the best way to keep the perimeter in sight. This fundamental FLIR tactic should be ingrained in all TFOs.

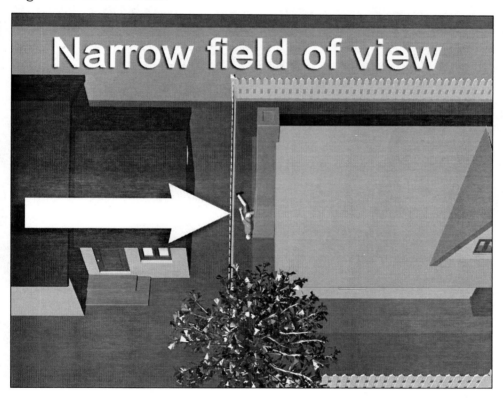

Figure 27. The arrow is pointing to a suspect who is lying down next to a house. A FLIR's narrow field of view should be used to search residential areas and to watch suspects closely.

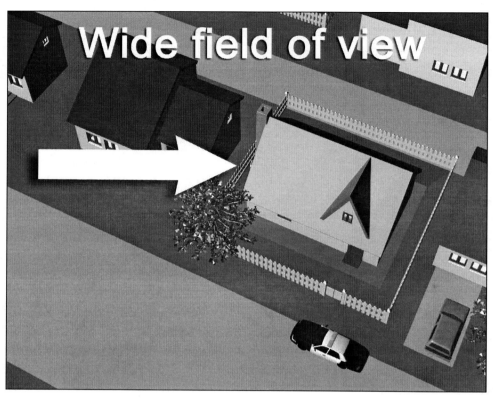

Figure 28. The arrow is pointing to a suspect behind a house. When an object is no longer visible in narrow field of view, the TFO should immediately switch to wide field of view. This is the fastest way to reacquire an object, and it is the best way to watch the perimeter.

Another option is to hover somewhere that enables the TFO to keep the object in sight at all times, but this should only be done if it can be done safely. It is usually not necessary to hover if the TFO uses the FLIR tactics described above.

There are some objects in backyards that can look like suspects who are hiding. Swimming pool pumps, large dogs, water heaters, etc. all generate a significant amount of heat. When a suspicious heat source is found, the TFO should study it for a moment to try and determine if it could be the suspect. If ground units are needed, the TFO should not hesitate to convey to them their concerns or opinions about the heat source, but they should never say that a heat source is the suspect unless they are absolutely sure.

When a suspicious heat source is found, the TFO should center it in the display, switch to wide field of view and make a mental note of where the object is in relation to other landmarks on the display. Then both crewmembers should glance outside for a moment and orient themselves to the object's location and to other officers and landmarks. The process of centering the object in the display and switching to wide field of view helps ensure that the FLIR does not drift off target while the aircrew is glancing outside.

The TFO should continue to watch the object in narrow field, but every ten seconds or so, he/she should switch to wide field of view for a moment. This helps the aircrew stay oriented while ground units are moving into the area.

Unless there are good reasons to do so, the TFO should not illuminate a suspicious heat source with the searchlight. Searchlights provide suspects with too much information. It is possible that they might surrender, but it is also possible, and very likely that they will run. It is much easier to direct ground units to a suspect who is hiding than to one who is running. Foot pursuits at night expose ground units to significant hazards and should be avoided when possible.

Officers who are familiar with FLIR search tactics understand the tactical drawbacks of illuminating suspects. When working with officers from other agencies, however, the aircrew might need to advise them against using the light if they request it at an inappropriate time. Ultimately, however, it is up to the officers on the ground to determine if and when they need the light.

DIRECTING OFFICERS TO HEAT SOURCES

Ground units are not always within the FLIR's field of view when a suspicious object is found, and the TFO may have to glance outside for a moment to see where the officers are. This is not necessarily the wrong thing to do, but the TFO should not spend too much time looking outside. The pilot can often see where the nearest ground units are and can usually provide the TFO with directions that get those officers closer to the heat source. When the TFO can see the officers and the heat source in the same field of view, it will be easier to direct them to a specific location.

A TFO should not spend any more time watching officers than is necessary. If a TFO focuses too much of his/her attention on the officers, at the expense of not being able to see the heat source, the suspect may move and the aircrew will not notice it.

When a TFO is directing officers to a specific building it is acceptable to use directions like "north, south, east, and west." When ground units get closer, however (in the same yard, for example), the TFO should use directions like, "straight ahead," or "to your right." Those directions are easier to understand and there is less chance for confusion.

Ground units need to know how far away they are from suspicious heat sources, but estimating distances can sometimes be difficult to do when looking at a FLIR display. If the TFO assumes that an average police officer is six feet tall, for example, he/she can estimate how far away the officers are from the heat source by counting how many officers it would take to fill the gap between them, and then multiply by six. This is not the most accurate method of estimating distances, but it is usually good enough to keep the ground units informed of their approximate distance from suspicious objects.

Ground units need to know exactly where a heat source is before they get to it, because it reduces the likelihood of them being surprised by the suspect. TFOs should also remember that as officers get closer to a suspect, the suspect may be able to hear their police radios.

TFOs need to speak clearly and concisely when directing officers to a heat source, and they must paint a verbal picture of exactly where the object is. This is one of the most overlooked and difficult skills for TFOs to master. Example:

> *The two officers with the canine unit are on the east side of the house. The heat source is in the backyard of that house. It's up against a fence, behind a shed at the northwest corner of the yard.*

Communicating in this manner not only identifies who the TFO is speaking to, but it helps ensure that everyone is correctly oriented to north, south, east, and west, and it also helps everyone understand where the heat source is in relation to them.

If a suspect is known to be armed, the TFO should not direct ground units to areas that are in close proximity to suspicious heat sources. Instead, they should direct officers to areas that provide them with adequate cover and concealment. The TFO then needs to ensure that the officers understand exactly where the heat source is so they do not approach it unknowingly. In those instances, officer safety might be enhanced by illuminating the suspect but only after the area has been contained, and only when officers are ready for the light. If a searchlight is used, it is very important that the light not illuminate the ground units. When officers are in good positions of cover around the heat source, a canine, SWAT team, or other tactical method of apprehending the suspect should be deployed first.

CANYON SEARCHES

When suspects flee into canyons, they either try to escape before a perimeter gets established or they hide. If ground units are going to conduct a search, they need to contain the area quickly.

Chasing armed suspects into a canyon at night is not a wise thing to do, especially when there is only one officer. Going into the canyon may be necessary, but it should be done in a more controlled manner with adequate cover and resources.

Suspects have a tactical advantage when they have evaded officers in a canyon. They know where the officers are, but the officers do not know where they are. That tactical advantage can be completely eliminated if air support arrives and finds the suspects before officers enter the canyon. It is probably going to take a few minutes for the aircrew to get to the scene, but as soon as they get the call, the TFO should ensure that a perimeter is being established.

There are two general types of perimeters: high profile and low profile, and officer safety should be the first consideration when deciding which one to use. Some other things to consider are the size of the canyon, the number of ground units available, the number of suspects and weapons, the severity of the crime, and the likelihood that the suspect is still in the canyon. Low-profile perimeters are used when air support is not available, or when a suspect has not been found after a thorough search. When setting up a low-profile perimeter, officers should stay out of sight and the helicopter should leave the immediate area. The goal is to make the suspect think that the officers are no longer searching.

If a canyon is relatively large, however, and officers believe that they have the suspect contained, it is often effective to set up a high-profile perimeter. This means that the perimeter units should turn on their vehicles' overhead lights and use their spotlights to illuminate the canyon rim. It is very important, however, that they not backlight or illuminate themselves, especially if the suspect is known to be armed. The goal is to make the suspect bush-in and hide until air support arrives to conduct a FLIR search. This is an effective tactic to use in large canyons when air support is available.

As the aircraft approaches the scene, the TFO should ask the ground units to point their flashlights directly at the helicopter. Once again, this helps the aircrew see the location of the tactical environment when they are a mile or more away. Once they know which canyon to search, the TFO should point the FLIR toward it as soon as possible. Suspects are going to hear the helicopter approaching, and they know that aircrews search with FLIR. If they think they can escape from the canyon before the helicopter arrives, they might try. To do this they are probably going to have to come out into the open and start running. If they do, they may be visible to ground units or to the FLIR operator, even from a distance. A warm moving object stands out well against a relatively cool stationary background.

If the suspects are not seen, the TFO should perform a quick initial scan of the entire canyon as soon as he/she arrives overhead. This initial scan is not an in-depth search; it is a quick overall scan, conducted in wide field of view. Its purpose is to see if there are any obvious heat sources that need to be looked at closer. When searching in wide field of view, the TFO should not move the imager so fast that he/she cannot see small heat sources. If the imager moves too fast, or has jerky movements, small but viable heat sources might be overlooked.

The TFO also needs to know if there are any officers in the canyon. It can be difficult to differentiate between officers and suspects with a FLIR. Oftentimes, the TFO is looking at how a person acts when trying to determine if that person is an officer or a suspect. If officers have already entered the canyon, it might not be practical to have them come back out. In those cases, the TFO needs to know exactly how many officers there are, and where they are. If practical, they should all group together and stay in one place to avoid being mistaken for suspects.

AIRCRAFT POSITIONING DURING CANYON SEARCHES

The orbit profile when searching a canyon is not always as critical as it is when searching residential areas, because there are not always as many obstacles for suspects to hide behind. Sometimes, however, the TFO's view is blocked by a thick canopy of trees and the pilot will have to change the aircraft's true angle from the tactical environment to enable the TFO to see underneath them. This can be done by descending, by increasing the aircraft's lateral offset, or a combination of both.

In Figure 29, Positions A and B provide the TFO with the same viewing angle of the tactical environment. Position A is preferable, however, because the aircraft is higher, which provides the aircrew with a greater margin of safety. The terrain, obstructions, and zooming capability of the FLIR will determine how far away the aircraft can be, yet still enable the FLIR to be effective.

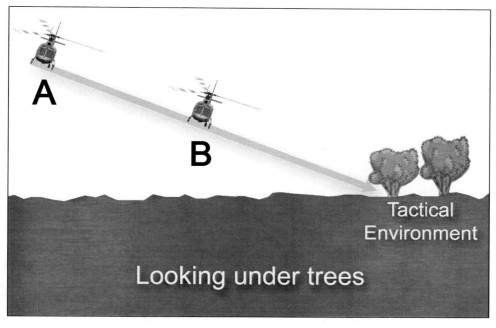

Figure 29. When trees block the TFO's view, the pilot will have to position the aircraft to enable the TFO to see under them. Pilots should always choose to fly as high as possible when doing this (Position A).

CANYON SEARCH TACTICS

When searching for suspects in canyons, the aircrew should initially search with FLIR and not the searchlight. The searchlight provides suspects with tactical information. It tells them exactly where the aircrew is searching, so they know when to move and when to hide. One tactic occasionally used is to point the searchlight in one direction while searching somewhere else with the FLIR. The theory is that the suspects might think the aircrew is searching where the light is pointed, and may move when it is not pointed at them. There is nothing necessarily wrong with this tactic, but it should not initially be used. If the searchlight accidentally illuminates the suspects while the aircrew is searching somewhere else with the FLIR, the suspects may start running and the aircrew will not see them.

There are some situations, however, when a searchlight might be more effective during a canyon search. When searching for a transient camp, for example, the light from the searchlight will often reflect off the trash, tarps, bicycles, and other items near the camp. Those reflections can often be seen at significant distances. The transients themselves, however, will likely be difficult to see.

It is important to distinguish between the two scenarios. When an aircrew is using a searchlight to look for a transient camp, they are not looking for a person; they are looking for objects that are associated with a person, objects that reflect visible light. When they are searching for a suspect with FLIR, however, they are looking for heat emissions from the person.

When conducting a FLIR search in a canyon, TFOs sometimes mistake rocks for suspects; not because their IQs are similar, but because their heat emissions can look similar. They both have relatively high heat emissions and well-defined edges, which are two of the three human infrared characteristics. It takes experience to become familiar with the differences, but it is something that can be learned.

There is also a noticeable difference between rocks on a west-facing slope and rocks on an east-facing slope. The rocks on a west-facing slope are exposed to the sun later into the afternoon so they will re-emit their heat later into the night. If the aircrew pays attention to all the rocks on a particular slope, they will notice that they all have similar heat emissions.

In many cases, a suspect is probably not going to look like a person at all. The only thing the aircrew may see is a small heat source under some bushes. There must be a direct, unobstructed line of sight between the suspect and the FLIR for the FLIR to be able to detect a suspect's heat emissions. If a suspect is completely concealed under dense brush, it is possible to avoid detection. Fortunately, when suspects hide in canyons, they are usually not able to completely conceal themselves. There are usually enough gaps between the branches and leaves that allow some of their body heat to escape.

When searching for suspects in canyons, tenacity and skill are often prerequisites for success. It may take several orbits around areas of dense brush before a TFO notices a suspicious heat source. That heat source may only have only one human infrared characteristic—relatively high heat emissions, but oftentimes that is all it takes.

SEARCHING DENSE BRUSH

When suspects hide in dense brush, they may only be visible to the FLIR operator for a few seconds at very narrow angles. Therefore, the TFO needs to search areas of dense brush in narrow field of view and from different angles. This means that the pilot will have to fly multiple orbits around a specific area to ensure that the TFO has enough time to conduct a thorough search.

When searching areas of dense brush, the search pattern should be similar to the pattern used when searching residential areas (Figure 30). Figure 30 is not to scale and is not meant to imply that only one orbit should be flown around areas of dense brush. It is intended to show the narrower search pattern that is used to search areas of dense brush versus areas that are more open. While orbiting areas of dense brush, the pilot should vary the circumference of the aircraft's orbit slightly to enable the TFO to search from different angles.

Some canyons do not have many obstructions, but suspects may still be able to conceal themselves from ground units simply by lying down in the darkness. In those environments, the TFO should scan the canyon in wide field of view as the pilot flies along the canyon's rim. Unlike areas of dense brush that require close inspection, a wide field of view is usually adequate for searching open areas. If a suspicious

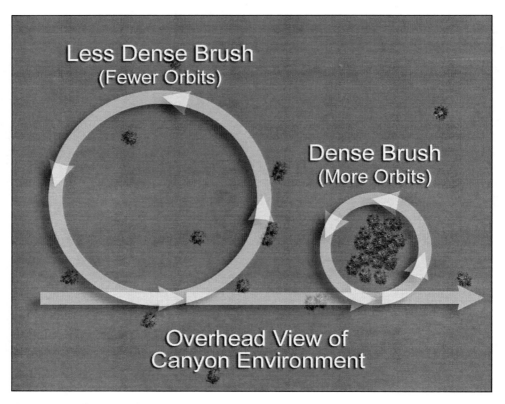

Figure 30. When searching areas of dense brush in a canyon, the aircraft's orbit profile should be narrower than it is when searching open areas.

heat source is found, the TFO can zoom in momentarily and study it closer. Open areas can be searched and cleared relatively quickly, so it is not necessary to fly the same search pattern as when searching areas of dense brush.

DAYTIME FLIR MISSIONS

Some believe that FLIR cannot be used in the daytime to search for hiding suspects. Older generation systems had less resolution than newer generation systems, and they weren't as sensitive to minor temperature differences. There are some limitations to daytime FLIR searches, but sometimes they can be very effective. One of the most difficult things to overcome is glare on the monitor. Reflections from outside the aircraft and from inside the cockpit can make it difficult to see small heat sources on the display.

Figure 31 is a FLIR image that was captured from a videotape of a daytime canyon search, and Figure 32 is a color camera image from the same search. Both images were taken within seconds of each other. The outside air temperature was 70 degrees, it was 08:40 hours, and the suspect was hiding near the bottom of a west-facing slope. The suspect's heat emissions are clearly visible on the FLIR image, but the suspect is not visible at all on the color camera image. The suspect also was not visible to the ground units, nor was he visible to the aircrew when they looked outside with binoculars. Aircrews need to remember that good FLIR search conditions do not only exist at night.

SEARCHING COMMERCIAL ROOFTOPS

It is not unusual for an aircrew to get called to search a rooftop when an alarm is activated or when someone reports suspicious activity. In many cases, officers will already have secured the perimeter, but they need the aircrew to search the roof.

As the aircraft approaches the scene, the TFO should acquire the building with the FLIR from as far away as possible. At significant distances, this might be difficult to do if there are not any obvious landmarks nearby. In those cases, it is helpful to have officers at the scene point their flashlights at the helicopter as it approaches.

Suspects on a roof are going to hear the helicopter approaching, and they are either going to run or hide. Air conditioners, heaters, and other rooftop-mounted equipment generate heat that can mask a person's body heat. None of that equipment moves across the roof, however, so the TFO should be looking for relatively high heat emissions and for movement.

As soon as the aircraft gets overhead, the TFO should glance outside at the rooftop for a moment with the naked eye. If a suspect has entered the building through an opening in the roof, light may be visible from inside the building. That light will contrast sharply with the dark surroundings and may be more noticeable than heat emissions from inside the building. Skylights can look like openings in a roof, but

Figure 31. The arrow is pointing to a suspect who was hiding in some dense brush. It was daytime and the suspect was found with the FLIR. He was not visible to the ground units, nor was he visible to the aircrew when they looked outside (Figure 32).

Figure 32. The arrow is pointing to a suspect who was hiding in some dense brush. In this daytime picture, the suspect is not visible. He was much easier to see with the FLIR, however, even though it was daytime (Figure 31).

if a business has skylights, there are usually more than one. A single hole in the roof will stand out relatively well if there is a light source behind it. If the TFO does not see anything visually, he/she should scan the roof with the FLIR and pay close attention to areas near heat-generating equipment.

Strip malls have several businesses under one common roof and TFOs should not limit their search to only the business in question. Suspects sometimes enter through a hole in the roof and crawl from business to business in the open area under the roof. It only takes a moment to search all of the rooftops.

When searching rooftops, the searchlight should not initially be used. When the light is turned on, suspects can see it. They might have time jump to another roof, conceal themselves, or run before the light illuminates them. Tactically, it is usually more effective to view the roof with the FLIR and the naked eye before using the searchlight. If nothing is seen, then the roof should be illuminated. If possible, the light should be pointed toward the roof before it is turned on.

When the TFO is illuminating the roof with the searchlight, he/she should also be using binoculars. If a suspect has entered a business through an opening in the roof and then covered the opening behind him/her, he/she may have left tools or other items on the roof. Those items may be small and may not generate much heat. They may be visible, however, when illuminated and viewed with binoculars (Figure 33).

The sequence of searching commercial rooftops in this manner is designed to maximize an aircrew's ability to find suspects without alerting the suspects that they have been found.

Figure 33. Searchlights should only be used to illuminate rooftops after a FLIR search has been conducted. Binoculars should be used in conjunction with the searchlight to look for small tools and other objects.

Chapter 6

INDOOR MARIJUANA CULTIVATION

Thermal imagers are very useful when trying to determine whether or not an indoor marijuana-grow is present in a building. High-intensity lamps are used by growers to simulate the sun. Those lamps and other electrical equipment generate a significant amount of heat (Figure 34). That heat must be vented or the plants will die.

Figure 34. High-intensity lamps and other electrical equipment are used at indoor marijuana grows. That equipment generates a significant amount of heat, which must be vented or the plants will die.

When an aircrew conducts a FLIR scan at a suspected indoor-grow, they are looking for heat anomalies that are commonly associated with indoor-grows; they are looking for abnormal heat emissions. It takes training and experience to be able to recognize those heat anomalies and to be able to articulate why they are unusual. Some indoor-grows have heat anomalies that are relatively easy to detect. Others, however, are less obvious.

The aircrew may conduct the FLIR scan, but it is entirely possible that someone else will interpret the image and offer an opinion as to whether or not an indoor-grow is present. The person who interprets the image is a thermographer and must have specific training to know what to look for.

LEGAL ISSUES

In the United States, the U.S. Supreme Court has ruled that a search warrant must be obtained before a FLIR scan of a residence can be conducted (*Kyllo v. United States* - 2001). Some investigators are unfamiliar with that ruling and may ask an aircrew to conduct a FLIR scan of a residence without a search warrant. Therefore, aircrews should always ensure that a search warrant has been obtained before they conduct a FLIR scan at a residence.

The law is not as clear, however, in regards to other types of structures. When in doubt, the investigator or the aircrew should discuss the issue with a prosecutor before conducting a FLIR scan. If a search warrant has been obtained, there is currently no case law that dictates at what altitude an aircraft must be flown when conducting the scan. Therefore, safety and tactical considerations should be the primary factors when determining what orbit profile to use.

ENVIRONMENTAL FACTORS

There is a variety of factors that affect how effective a FLIR scan will be. Solar loading, for example, is a phenomenon that significantly affects how a structure will look when viewed with a FLIR. When structures are exposed to the sun, they absorb infrared energy until

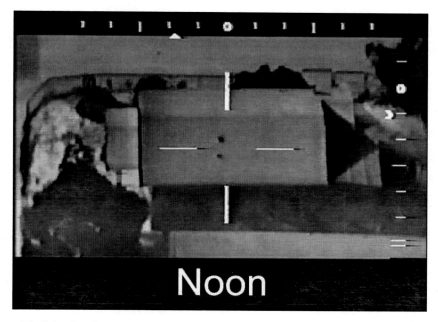

Figure 35. Solar loading is a phenomenon that occurs when objects are exposed to the sun. This house has absorbed a significant amount of infrared energy from the sun, and the FLIR operator will probably not be able to detect heat anomalies that are generated from inside the structure.

Figure 36. When a structure has not been exposed to the sun for several hours, heat emissions, generated from inside the structure will probably be visible to the FLIR operator.

their surfaces reach their peak absorption levels. Those surfaces then re-emit that heat as the sun sets. This is usually not a problem unless the TFO is trying to detect heat emissions that are being generated from inside the structure.

Figures 35 and 36 are of the same residence. Figure 35 was scanned at about noon when the outside air temperature was approximately 75 degrees. Figure 36 was scanned at about midnight when the outside air temperature was about 55 degrees. In Figure 35, it would be very difficult to identify heat emissions that were being generated from inside the structure. Solar loading would mask most, if not all of those heat emissions. In Figure 36, however, solar loading is no longer a factor, and heat anomalies that are consistent with an indoor grow would probably be visible. Therefore, when scanning a suspected indoor-grow, the aircrew should wait until the structure has emitted most of the infrared energy that it absorbed from the sun during the day. Only then will a thermographer be able to determine if the structure's heat emissions are consistent with an indoor-grow.

It is impossible to say at exactly what time a FLIR scan can be conducted, because several factors will affect the quality of the image. Generally speaking, a FLIR scan of a suspected indoor marijuana-grow can be conducted anytime after midnight, because most of the heat that the structure absorbed from the sun should be gone.

Rain, fog, and heavy mist conditions should be avoided when conducting FLIR scans, because water vapor attenuates heat which reduces the quality of the image. A FLIR scan is a qualitative analysis, and a thermographer needs to see as many details as possible when evaluating an image.

THE BRIEFING

The TFO should speak with the investigator or case agent, prior to conducting the FLIR scan. Everyone needs to understand how the mission will be conducted and that no opinion as to the presence of an indoor-grow will be offered over the radio unless there is an immediate need to do so. The mission should be conducted on a tactical frequency if possible, and the location of the suspected grow should not be broadcast over the radio. A video recording of the FLIR scan should be made for analysis at a later time, and for evidentiary purposes.

When conducting FLIR scans, TFOs should not focus too much of their attention on evaluating the image. Instead, they should be trying to acquire good video of the structure for a more thorough analysis at a later time. Some indoor-grow heat anomalies are obvious, while others are more difficult to notice on the small monitors typically found in helicopters. It is also possible for thermographers to mistake a heat anomaly that they believe to be consistent with an indoor-grow for one that is generated by a legitimate heat source. So while it may be tempting for thermographers to offer opinions based on what they see in the aircraft, it is usually a better idea to review the recording at a later time, on a larger monitor under more relaxed conditions.

RESIDENTIAL AREA FLIR SCANS

When conditions are suitable for a FLIR scan, the TFO should tell the investigator to go to a location that is roughly two miles from the suspected-grow. The aircrew needs to rendezvous with them at a location that would not arouse suspicion if the suspect were to drive by. When the aircrew arrives overhead, the TFO should locate the investigator's vehicle with the FLIR and activate the video recorder. The TFO should tell the investigator that the recorder is on and that they are ready to proceed.

The TFO should keep the FLIR pointed at the investigator's vehicle as the investigator drives to the suspected-grow. While en route, the TFO should record the following audio information: the aircrew's names, the date, time, the outside air temperature, the general location of the FLIR scan, and the aircraft's altitude. If audio cannot be recorded, those details should be written down and attached in some manner to the recording when it is impounded. The original recording should always be impounded as evidence, even if the FLIR scan is inconclusive. No opinions or comments about scan should be recorded.

When the investigator is directly in front of the residence, they should stop for a moment and tell the TFO that the house is off to their right or left, for example. When the TFO understands exactly which structure to scan, they should tell the investigator that it is okay to leave.

It may not be reasonable or prudent for an investigator to stop directly in front of a suspected-grow, especially if someone is standing outside. In those cases, the TFO should be prepared to locate the structure as the investigator drives by and describes it. If the TFO is ever unsure about which structure they are supposed to scan, they need to clarify it immediately.

Residences that are located in isolated areas will often require a more in-depth briefing to ensure that the aircrew understands exactly which house needs to be scanned. Aerial photos from an inconspicuous altitude are an excellent way of identifying the specific structure, but a FLIR should not be used to acquire those images. That may be interpreted as conducting a FLIR scan, which requires a search warrant. If a search warrant has been obtained to conduct a FLIR scan, scanning the residence with a FLIR to point out its location to the aircrew may be interpreted as the actual execution of that search warrant.

AIRCRAFT POSITIONING DURING FLIR SCANS

The pilot needs to ensure that the FLIR has an obstructed view of all sides of the structure, if possible. When conducting a FLIR scan, the aircraft's orbit profile will be very similar to when the aircrew is searching for suspects in residential areas. A good orbit profile to use is to fly at approximately 30 knots, at about 600 feet AGL, with a lateral offset of about three-quarters of a block. Newer generation FLIRs will enable the aircraft to be flown higher with a similar view of the structure.

Figure 37 is a still shot, captured from a videotape of an indoor-grow. The elevation symbology indicates a 40 degree down angle, which is similar to when searching for suspects in residential areas. This orbit profile gives the TFO an unobstructed view of the roof and all sides of the structure as the aircraft orbits. It should take no more than two orbits to acquire adequate video of a structure from different angles. If the aircrew spends too much time overhead, the occupants may get suspicious of what the aircrew is doing.

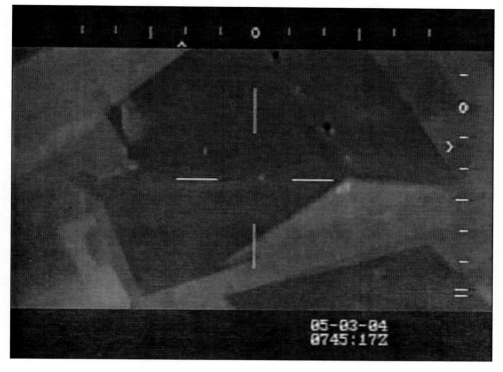

Figure 37. Several heat anomalies that are consistent with an indoor-marijuana grow are visible in this picture. The roof has warm patchy areas, the vent at the peak of the roof is unusually warm, and the wall adjacent to the attic is warm.

CONDUCTING THE FLIR SCAN

Roughly 80 to 90 percent of the FLIR scan should be conducted in narrow field of view with occasional shots from a wide field of view. This gives the thermographer the best view of any heat anomalies that might be present.

There are several publications that teach people how to grow marijuana indoors and those same publications talk about law enforcement investigative tactics, including the use of FLIR. If a suspect comes outside while the FLIR scan is being conducted, the aircrew should be prepared to use tactics that throw suspicion off their true mission. For example, prior to conducting a FLIR scan, the TFO should position the searchlight so it is pointed in a different direction than the FLIR. If a suspect comes outside, the light can be turned on to illuminate something somewhere else. The ruse is more believable if the search-light is being moved around, but it should not be rapidly sweeping across the rooftops of houses because it would not be believable.

Another tactic is to orbit the house a short distance away after the FLIR scan has been conducted. These orbits should be visible to the suspect about a block or so away. The goal is to make the suspect think that the aircrew is searching for something in the general area. It may help add to the illusion if the searchlight is turned on and is pointed at something for a few moments. This is a very effective tactic, especial-ly if it is not uncommon for the helicopter to be in the area.

The aircrew needs to remember that residents in the area, including the suspect, may call the police and ask what the helicopter is doing. The dispatchers should be prepared to give them a false answer.

HEAT ANOMALIES

There are some heat anomalies that are fairly common to residences that have indoor-grows; however, suspects sometimes go to great lengths to hide the vented heat. In those cases, the thermographer might not see anything, or he/she might see something that looks com-pletely different.

In Figure 37, several heat anomalies, which are fairly common to indoor-grows are present. For example, the wall adjacent the attic is noticeably warmer than the wall below it, the attic vent under the peak of the roof is unusually warm and warm patchy areas can be seen on the roof. These heat anomalies are not always present, but they are fairly common to indoor-grows.

Thermographers need to be careful when scanning older homes. Older homes often have less insulation than newer homes, and addi-tions to the structure may have been built on over time. The newer sections may be better insulated, which will make the older sections look warmer. It can be easy to mistake those warmer sections for indoor-grow heat anomalies. It is also not uncommon for garages to be noticeably warmer than the rest of the house, because garages are not always insulated.

Thermographers also need to be aware of the effects of trees and other foliage near the house. Trees emit heat to varying degrees. If a tree is right next to a house, for example, and its leaves overhang the roof, heat emissions from the tree will be absorbed by the structure and then re-emitted. That heat can look very similar to the warm patchy heat anomalies that are commonly found at indoor-grows.

Thermographers should not refer to heat anomalies as "heat signatures." A signature is something that is unique to a specific item or person, and heat anomalies that are consistent with indoor-grows are not always unique enough to constitute a signature. A FLIR scan is a qualitative analysis, not a quantitative analysis. Therefore, it is not possible to say with 100 percent certainty that a particular heat anomaly is only associated with an indoor marijuana-grow. Other legal activities can produce similar heat emissions.

A FLIR scan should be used to augment a thorough investigation and should not normally be relied upon as the sole basis for obtaining a search warrant. However, experienced thermographers can be relied upon heavily for their opinions.

It takes specific training and experience to evaluate FLIR scans consistently. A good practice for thermographers is to avoid learning other details about the case until after they form an opinion based solely on the FLIR scan. The Thermographer's opinion should be objective and should not be influenced by other factors related to the case.

Chapter 7

VEHICLE PURSUITS

Law enforcement helicopters are often referred to as "force multipliers," because an experienced, well equipped aircrew can perform missions that would otherwise require many additional ground units. For example, during a vehicle pursuit, it is usually much safer and far easier for an aircrew to keep a fleeing suspect in sight than it is for a dozen ground units. An aircrew might not be able to physically apprehend a suspect, but they can certainly enhance the ability of ground units to do so.

AIRCREW DUTIES DURING PURSUITS

An aircrew can, and should, do much more than simply watch a pursuit. Good aircrew tactics and pursuit skills can minimize the dangers to officers and citizens and can significantly increase the likelihood of apprehending suspects. One of the most important things a TFO can do to enhance safety during a pursuit is use a calm voice when talking on the radio. This has a tremendous calming effect on other officers. If the pursuing officers believe that the pursuit is under control, and that the suspect is not going to get away, they tend to drive slower and take fewer risks. They are able to concentrate more on their driving and less on keeping the suspect in sight. The end result is a safer pursuit.

A pursuit may last for two minutes or for two hours. A suspect might stay in one neighborhood and never exceed 40 mph, or he/she might cross state lines and drive in excess of 100 mph. If the pursuit occurs in an area that the aircrew is familiar with, and if the pilot doesn't have to deal with congested airspace or inclement weather, their workload will be fairly predictable. Under those conditions, an experienced pilot should be able to assist the TFO by providing the names of approaching cross streets and traffic conditions ahead of the pursuit. However, if the pilot is less experienced, or must deal with other issues, he/she may not be able to assist the TFO at all. It is important to emphasize that pilots should not be providing TFOs with this information unless it is needed, and only then when it is safe and reasonable to do so.

The TFO should be "calling the pursuit," which means he/she should be providing ground units, supervisors, and dispatchers with information about the pursuit. Pertinent information like the pursuit's location, the vehicle's speed, how the suspect is driving, traffic conditions, and any other information is helpful. TFOs should not attempt to "clear intersections," that is, they should not tell the pursuing officers that an intersection has no opposing traffic or hazards. It is not always possible for TFOs to see pedestrians or other vehicles that might be present.

When less experienced ground units get involved in pursuits, they often have difficulty relinquishing the duty of calling the pursuit. It is very important, however, that the TFO assume those duties as soon as possible, because it reduces the workload of ground units. Sometimes it might even be necessary for the TFO to get on the radio and tell the pursuing officers that the aircrew will call the pursuit and the ground units should concentrate on their driving.

It is not unusual for a pursuit to enter a neighboring city or an area that the aircrew is unfamiliar with. If neither crewmember knows the names of the streets, the TFO might be able to read street signs with binoculars, but the TFO should not use binoculars during most of the pursuit. There is too much peripheral information outside their field of view that can affect the safety of officers and citizens. If the aircraft is equipped with a moving map, the names of the streets can often be read right off the display. Workload permitting, the pilot may even be able to read them and provide them to the TFO. This frees up the TFO so he/she can pay more attention to the pursuit itself.

If the aircrew does not know the names of the streets in the area, the TFO should instruct the second ground unit in the pursuit to call out the name of the street but nothing more. The TFO should continue to provide everyone with the pursuit's location, its direction of travel, the vehicle's speed, traffic conditions, etc. Providing this information does more than just answer those questions; it reassures everyone that the pursuit is under control and that the suspect is not going to get away. If the TFO stops providing that information, simply because he/she does not know the names of the streets, the ground units will start calling the pursuit themselves. They will feel the need to drive faster and to take additional risks to keep the suspect in sight. When TFOs are no longer calling the pursuit, and are simply watching or recording it, the safety benefits of the helicopter are lost.

VIDEO RECORDING PURSUITS IN THE DAYTIME

A video recording has significant evidentiary and tactical value. Pursuits and other incidents can be reviewed to see what suspects did, where they hid, or where they discarded evidence. It takes a considerable amount of skill and practice, however, to be able to operate a camera system during a pursuit. Most pursuits can be recorded simply by setting the camera in wide field of view and pointing it in the general direction of the vehicle. If the pilot positions the aircraft effectively, most of the pursuit will be recorded.

Manually controlling the camera during a daytime pursuit should only be attempted by experienced TFOs who are proficient with their equipment. The skills needed to manipulate a camera while calling a pursuit can (and should) be learned, but it takes a considerable amount of practice. Those skills need to be in place before they are needed, not attempted for the first time when they are needed. The safe conduct of a pursuit is a higher priority than the need to record it. Safety can be enhanced by the TFO looking outside and calling the pursuit, but experienced TFOs should never use "safety" as an excuse for not being proficient with their tactical equipment.

Experienced and proficient TFOs can usually manipulate a camera system while simultaneously calling a pursuit. Good aircrew coordination skills are important, because the camera has a limited field of view and the TFO may occasionally need help from the pilot. For example, pilots may be able to provide TFOs with the names of cross streets or with traffic conditions ahead of the pursuit. The TFO would then relay that information to ground units. The pilot's attention should be focused outside during most of a pursuit, and traffic conditions and cross streets are fairly easy for them to see. It is important to emphasize that pilots should only provide such information when it is needed, and only if their workload permits.

TFOs should not focus their attention solely on the display during a pursuit, because it precludes them from seeing things peripherally, and it is more difficult for them to stay oriented. Instead, they should glance back and forth between what they see on the display and what they see outside. The ratio of how often to look inside versus outside will change as conditions change. For example, as the TFO zooms in on a vehicle with the camera his/her workload will increase proportionately. He/she will need to concentrate more on the display and on manipulating the camera, which means he/she will have less time to look outside. Sometimes it might be helpful to zoom in on something, but it usually is not necessary. When suspects are rapidly changing directions, or if the aircraft is maneuvering sharply, it is much more difficult for the TFO to keep the camera pointed at a vehicle if the camera is zoomed in closely. A camera's field of view should be framed so that it captures the overall incident.

During a pursuit, the pilot should focus his/her attention outside the cockpit as much as possible. Sometimes, however, the pilot may lose sight of the vehicle behind the airframe or the instrument panel. The left side of the instrument panel rises when the aircraft rolls to the right, and it might block the pilot's view of the vehicle. This happens when the aircraft is too close behind the vehicle or when it is too high. When that happens, the pilot should be able to glance down at the display for a moment, to keep the vehicle in sight. This will help the pilot keep the aircraft positioned effectively in case the suspect stops or turns.

If the TFO is using the camera to record a pursuit, the pilot needs to ensure that the camera's view of the fleeing vehicle is not blocked by the airframe. The best way to do that is to become familiar with areas of the aircraft's windscreen that give the pilot a good view of the vehicle, while simultaneously enabling the camera and TFO to see it outside. That way, the vehicle will always be visible if the pilot keeps it in the same relative position to the aircraft.

AIRCRAFT POSITIONING DURING FREEWAY PURSUITS

Vehicle pursuits can be broken down into two basic categories: higher-speed freeway pursuits and lower speed residential area pursuits. This does not mean that all freeway pursuits are high speed, nor does it mean that pursuits in residential areas are always slower than freeway pursuits. A vehicle's speed and the pursuit environment are used to distinguish between the two types of pursuits, because those factors will determine how the pilot positions the aircraft.

One of the most common mistakes that pilots make during pursuits is to allow the aircraft to get too close to the vehicle. When that happens they lose sight of the vehicle behind the instrument panel or the airframe. If the TFO is not using the camera or FLIR, the suspect will be able to stop and flee on foot and neither crewmember may see it. To prevent this from happening, pilots should resist the temptation to get too close behind the vehicle, or to fly alongside it. The only time the aircraft should be positioned alongside a vehicle during a pursuit is when the vehicle is turning, going relatively slow, or has stopped.

Figure 38. This picture is a diagram of aircraft positioning when pursuing vehicles at different speeds. Generally speaking, the slower a vehicle goes, the closer the aircraft should be to it.

Generally speaking, the faster a vehicle is going, the higher and farther back the aircraft should fly. This will give the pilot more time to react when the suspect turns, stops, or exits the freeway quickly, and the pilot's workload will be reduced. The picture in Figure 38 was taken from the pilot's seat of a helicopter at 600 feet AGL. The numbers represent an approximation of where a vehicle should be positioned in relation to the aircraft at different speeds. Figure 39 is a diagram of aircraft positioning when a vehicle is going 80 mph or faster. A good pursuit profile to use during higher speed freeway pursuits is to fly at an altitude of approximately 600 feet AGL, about the length of two city blocks behind the vehicle and slightly offset to the right. If the pilot flies from the left seat, this offset would be reversed. As the vehicle slows down, the distance between it and the aircraft should be reduced. This will enable the pilot to perform turns around the vehicle when the suspect changes directions.

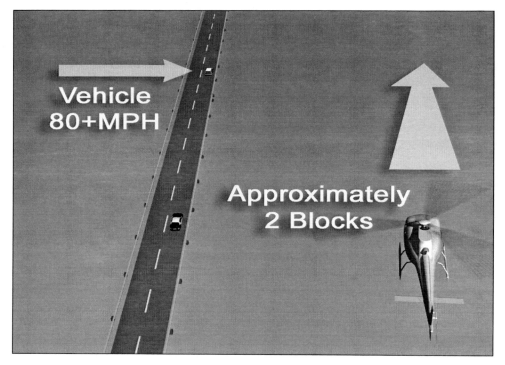

Figure 39. When an aircrew is pursuing a high-speed vehicle on a freeway, the aircraft should be flown at a distance of about the length of two city blocks behind it. This gives the pilot time to react if the suspect stops, turns, or exits the freeway quickly.

Aircrews should experiment with flying even higher during vehicle pursuits. For example, when flying at 1000 feet AGL the pilot's workload will be significantly less than when flying at 600 feet AGL, and there are fewer ground-based obstructions. The latest generation of camera systems can zoom in well enough for aircrews to keep suspects in sight at 1000 feet AGL, even if they flee on foot. If aircrews are going to fly at higher altitudes, however, TFOs must be very proficient with the camera system or FLIR because the pilot is going to be referring to the display more often to keep the aircraft positioned effectively. Flying at higher altitudes has its benefits, but it also requires a higher degree of crew coordination and technical proficiency.

AIRCRAFT POSITIONING DURING RESIDENTIAL AREA PURSUITS

When a vehicle is being pursued in a residential area, the aircraft should be flown somewhat lower and closer to the vehicle than during a freeway pursuit. Suspects can turn and stop much faster when they are going slower, which gives them a greater ability to turn into alleys or to stop behind buildings and other obstructions.

A good pursuit profile to use during residential area pursuits is to fly at approximately 450 feet AGL, with a lateral offset of about one-half to three-quarters of a block, and the same distance behind the vehicle (Figure 40). This puts the aircraft at about a 45 degree offset behind the vehicle.

When suspects change directions in residential areas, they usually make 90, or 180 degree turns, because that is the way most residential streets and alleys are laid out. That is not always the case, but it is more common than not. If the aircraft is too low, too far back, or if it has too much lateral offset, the suspect may be able to stop and bail out of the vehicle behind an obstruction before the aircrew is close enough to see them. Then it may be difficult or impossible to find or identify the driver.

Figure 40: When pursuing vehicles in residential areas, the aircraft should be flown at about 450 feet AGL, about one-half, to three-quarters of a block behind and to the right of the vehicle.

MANEUVERING DURING RESIDENTIAL AREA PURSUITS

When suspects make right 90 degree turns, it is tempting to make a right 90 degree turn to stay with them, but this is not an effective maneuver. When the aircraft turns right it also rolls to the right, which will cause both crewmembers to lose sight of the vehicle behind the airframe. If the suspect stops, or makes another right turn while the aircraft is banked to the right, neither crewmember is going to be able to see it, nor will they be able to see if someone bails out of the vehicle.

A more effective tactic is to make a very slight, but quick initial right turn immediately after the suspect commits to making a right turn (Figure 41, Position A). The pilot should cross in front of the vehicle's path and enter a left 270 degree turn around it (Figure 41, Position B). During this part of the maneuver, the aircraft will be going in the opposite direction of the vehicle. That is normal and is why an initial right turn is built into the maneuver. It increases the aircraft's lateral offset distance from the vehicle as they converge. This enables the aircrew to be far enough away from the vehicle to avoid overflying it, yet still be able to see it. If the pilot pays close attention to aircraft positioning, the helicopter will stay in the same relative position to the vehicle throughout the turn and both crewmembers will be able to keep it in sight.

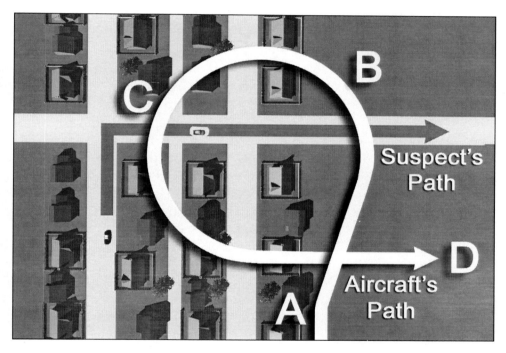

Figure 41. When suspects make right turns in front of the helicopter, the pilot should make a slight, but quick initial right turn, and then perform a left 270 degree turn around the vehicle. This will keep the aircraft positioned effectively.

If the suspect makes another right turn while the aircraft is maneuvering, the pilot would simply roll out of the turn 90 degrees sooner, and the aircraft would be perfectly positioned to continue the pursuit. If the suspect makes a left turn while the aircraft is maneuvering, the pilot would continue turning through 360 degrees. Once again, the aircraft would be in a good position to continue the pursuit. If the suspect stops and bails out at any time during this maneuver, the aircrew will be in a good position to see it.

PURSUING MOTORCYCLES

Motorcycle pursuits often pose the greatest challenges to aircrews. Some motorcycles are capable of going more than 160 mph and few helicopters can fly that fast. Freeway pursuits at those speeds are often nothing more than a drag race. The only tactics that might be effective would be to climb so the TFO can keep the suspect in sight with binoculars, and position ground units ahead of the pursuit. When motorcycles enter residential areas or business districts, however, it is usually more difficult for them to outrun the helicopter if the pilot uses good pursuit tactics.

Motorcycles are capable of stopping, accelerating, and turning much faster than most cars, and the riders can often tell when the helicopter is out of position. They might choose that time to stop behind an obstruction and flee on foot. There are some tactics that the pilot can use, however, to keep the aircraft positioned effectively. For example, if it looks like the suspect is an experienced rider or is driving unusually fast, the pilot should fly the pursuit somewhat higher and farther back (between 500 and 600 feet AGL). This will compensate somewhat for the motorcycle's ability to pull ahead when it comes out of a turn.

The maneuver in Figure 41 is typically flown at a fairly constant altitude of about 450 feet AGL, but it should be flown somewhat higher when pursuing high-speed motorcycles. The pilot should also modify the aircraft's altitude throughout the maneuver to enable the helicopter to accelerate faster when it comes out of the turn. If the motorcycle makes a right turn in front of the helicopter, for example, the pilot should perform the same left 270 degree turn, but as the aircraft approaches Position B, the pilot should initiate a shallow climb. This will help reduce the lateral circumference of the turn, which helps keep the aircraft closer to the motorcycle. As the helicopter approaches Position C, the pilot should nose the aircraft down and accelerate quickly by trading altitude for airspeed (Figure 42).

It is very important to emphasize that the aircraft should never be brought to a hover or slowed excessively when performing these maneuvers. These maneuvers are not pedal turns; they are tight turns that allow the pilot to maintain as much forward airspeed as possible. Pursuit flying is energy management, and much of that energy is stored in the forward motion of the aircraft.

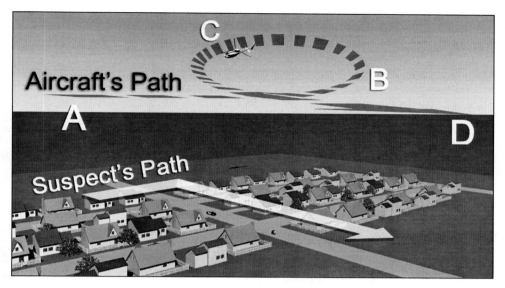

Figure 42. When motorcycles and other high-speed vehicles make right turns in front of the aircraft, the pilot should enter a left 270 turn around the vehicle and initiate a shallow climb. The pilot can accelerate quickly when coming out of the turn by descending. This will help the pilot keep the aircraft positioned effectively.

OVERRUNNING VEHICLES

Many vehicles are capable of accelerating and decelerating at faster rates than a helicopter in level flight. Sometimes suspects will slow down quickly in residential areas and the aircraft will overrun them. When that happens the pilot is probably going to lose sight of the vehicle behind the airframe unless quick action is taken. Pilots should resist the temptation to slow down by performing a "quick stop," because the aircraft will be exposed to abrupt power and attitude changes, which may cause it to get too slow. Instead, forward airspeed should be maintained at all times and the pilot should perform a left 360 degree turn around the vehicle. When performing this turn, both crewmembers should be able to keep the vehicle in sight at all times. Essentially, this is the same maneuver as depicted in Figure 41.

If the aircraft overruns a vehicle that is going 80 mph or faster, a 360 degree turn should not be performed. The time spent flying in the opposite direction, and the reduction in airspeed induced by the turn will cause the helicopter to get too far behind the vehicle. In those cases, the pilot should slow down by reducing power, and let the vehicle pull ahead. Some helicopters are not capable of flying faster than about 85 knots in level flight. In those cases, the referenced speeds should be reduced proportionately.

When maneuvering over a pursuit, pilots sometimes inadvertently allow the aircraft to descend, which causes their workload to increase significantly. As the aircraft gets closer to the vehicle, changes in their relative positions become more pronounced and occur faster. The closer the aircraft gets to the vehicle, the more difficult it will be for the pilot to keep the aircraft in the same relative position. Pilots will find themselves "yanking and banking" much more at lower altitudes than at higher altitudes.

NIGHTTIME VEHICLE PURSUITS

When pursuing vehicles at night, the pilot should use the same aircraft positioning techniques and maneuvering tactics as when pursuing vehicles in the daytime. Vehicle pursuits often end in foot pursuits and at night it is much more difficult for an aircrew to keep a suspect in sight when they flee on foot than it is in the daytime. Therefore, the TFO should be using the FLIR during nighttime vehicle pursuits. When using the FLIR, the TFO should glance back and forth between what is seen outside and what is seen on the display. This will help the TFO stay oriented and it will be easier to call the pursuit.

Some agencies prioritize the searchlight during nighttime vehicle pursuits. They feel that the light may alert citizens to the oncoming pursuit and intimidate the fleeing suspect. Some suspects may pull over and surrender, but most will not. The overwhelming majority of them will continue to flee whether they are being illuminated or not.

The benefits of illuminating vehicles during pursuits are questionable, but they can be achieved without surrendering the tactical and safety benefits of using the FLIR. For example, the searchlight could be positioned so that it illuminates the vehicle during most of the pursuit. As long as the pilot positions the aircraft effectively, the light will illuminate the vehicle and citizens will still be able to see it. If the pilot can control the searchlight with controls mounted on the cyclic or collective, it will be fairly easy to keep the light in position. It will also free up the TFO so he/she can use the FLIR, which is far more effective during nighttime operations.

It takes practice to become proficient with the FLIR during nighttime vehicle pursuits, and it requires a higher degree of crew coordination than when the TFO is using a searchlight. That is why some aircrews shy away from the use of FLIR during a pursuit. If those crew coordination and FLIR skills can be mastered, however, the aircrew will be far more effective.

TRACKING VEHICLES

When a pursuit gets terminated, and ground units are no longer chasing the suspect, aircrews often get tasked with "tracking" the vehicle. The purpose of tracking a vehicle is to take the pressure off the suspect so he/she will slow down and not drive as recklessly. If the aircrew can keep the vehicle in sight they can sometimes direct ground units to the suspect(s) when they stop and flee on foot.

When ground units are no longer behind the suspect, the aircrew should continue to follow the vehicle at an inconspicuous altitude and distance, and the TFO should be keeping other officers informed of the suspect's location. At night, the searchlight should be turned off, because it defeats the purpose of tracking a vehicle. Hopefully, the suspect will slow down and abandon the vehicle, and the TFO will be able to direct officers to the suspect's location.

Suspects usually know when a helicopter is overhead during a pursuit. When ground units drop off, it is not realistic to assume that a suspect will believe that the helicopter has also dropped off. Some suspects may slow down, but others will continue to flee or drive even faster. They might even turn off their lights to avoid being seen. There is no way of knowing what they will do.

It might be a good idea to try tracking a suspect under certain conditions, but the aircrew must pay close attention to what a suspect does when ground units drop off. If the suspect continues to drive erratically, it might be necessary to have the ground units re-engage in the pursuit. A police car's siren and emergency lights provide citizens with at least some warning of the hazardous situation.

If the helicopter is too far away from the vehicle while tracking it, it can be difficult for the aircrew to keep it in sight, especially at night.

This is another reason why TFOs should become proficient with their FLIR skills. It is much easier to keep a vehicle or a suspect in sight at night with the FLIR than with the naked eye.

Tracking a vehicle might work in some situations, and it might be necessary to try in others, but it is not always the most effective tactic. Inclement weather may preclude the aircrew from being able to enter Class D airspace, or to track the vehicle at all. When operating near the localizer of an airport, the pilot might not be able to stay with the pursuit if another aircraft is on an approach. Therefore, aircrews need to coordinate the process of tracking a vehicle with supervisors and ground units before ground units drop off.

Chapter 8

FOOT PURSUITS

DAYTIME FOOT PURSUITS

Suspects run from officers for a variety of reasons. If a TFO hears something on the radio that makes him/her believe that a suspect is about to run, he/she should tell the ground units to delay their contact with that person for as long as possible. This will give the aircrew more time to move into the area. It is much easier for an aircrew to follow someone who is running than it is to find them once they have hidden.

When an aircrew gets involved in a daytime foot pursuit the pilot should position the aircraft so both crewmembers can see the suspect outside 90 degrees to the left (or to the right if pilots fly from the left seat). The pilot should maintain forward airspeed at all times and orbit at a safe altitude around the suspect.

Some pilots fly extremely low when pursuing suspects on foot. Sometimes they are so low that it looks like they are trying to herd the suspects with the helicopter, or spear them with the aircraft's wire-strike kit. That may seem like an exaggeration, but the fact is that some law enforcement helicopters have been downed by suspects throwing rocks. A good orbit profile to use during daytime foot pursuits is to fly at approximately 40 knots, at about 400 feet AGL, with a one-quarter block lateral offset from the suspect. At this airspeed, altitude, and distance, the aircraft will have enough angle of bank for the pilot to see past the TFO, and the TFO should have a good view of the suspect. Pilots should not hover during foot pursuits unless there is a reason to and only then if it is safe to do so. When hovering, the aircraft loses its angle of bank, which makes it more difficult for the pilot to see past the TFO.

A suspect may be able to hide from the aircrew, but if the aircrew is watching the suspect closely, and has a good view of the perimeter, they can ensure that the suspect cannot escape. The aircrew might not be able to see the suspect, but knowing where the suspect is, is the next best thing.

It is very easy for pilots to focus too much on a foot pursuit and not pay enough attention to what is going on with the aircraft, but it is very important that they fly the aircraft first.

NIGHTTIME FOOT PURSUITS

Some aircrews prioritize the FLIR during nighttime foot pursuits while others use a searchlight. Searchlights are easier to use and require fewer crew coordination skills than when using a FLIR. Searchlights, however, have significant tactical drawbacks and there are some safety issues that need to be considered when using them. For example, Figure 43 is a still image that was captured from a video-tape during a foot pursuit. The FLIR image was being recorded, but the TFO was using a searchlight to illuminate the suspect. The Bell 206 was in a left hand orbit at about 300 feet AGL, and both crewmembers were watching the suspect outside 90 degrees to the left. This is a fairly common method of positioning an aircraft during a foot pursuit when a searchlight is being used.

In Figure 43, the azimuth symbology indicates that the FLIR is pointed almost straight ahead, and a MD 500 can be seen in the upper left corner of the picture. This is another law enforcement helicopter that was involved in the same incident. Both aircraft were in Class B airspace, but through a series of communication errors, neither pilot knew the other was there. The pilot of the Bell 206 did not see the MD 500 until it passed by them on the left, approximately 75 feet away.

Neither pilot saw the other aircraft, because their priorities were misplaced. Beyond the obvious interagency communication issues, the aircrews were focused too much on the mission and not enough on safety of flight. Both crewmembers in the Bell 206 were looking outside 90 degrees to the left, which made it very difficult for them to see

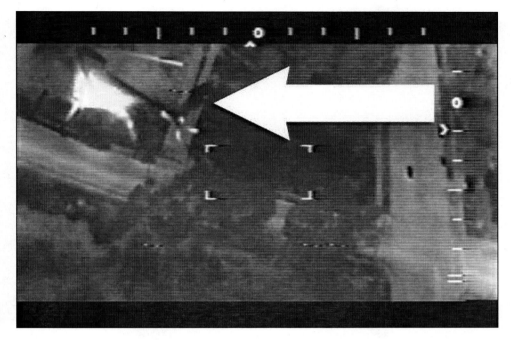

Figure 43. The MD 500 in the upper left corner of this photo was nearly hit by the Bell 206 that recorded this image. Both crewmembers in the Bell 206 were looking outside, 90 degrees to the left, illuminating a suspect with the searchlight.

what was in front of their aircraft. This is a common problem when a searchlight is used to illuminate something on the inside of an orbit, especially if that object is moving. The pilot has to spend a considerable amount of time looking in that direction to position the aircraft effectively. If both crewmembers had been looking at the FLIR display, however, they would likely have noticed the other helicopter in their peripheral vision before it became a hazard. The FLIR display is more in line with the aircraft's direction of flight so objects in front of the aircraft are easier to see.

When illuminating a suspect during a foot pursuit, the aircraft usually has to be flown relatively low for both crewmembers to be able to see the suspect. When pilots attempt to fly higher, they have to fly a wider orbit profile so they can see past the TFO. A wider orbit profile makes it more difficult for the aircrew to see the suspect, because the aircraft is farther away and it is dark. Wider orbit profiles also enable suspects to hide behind obstructions easier.

Another option when using a searchlight is to fly faster with an increased angle of bank, which enables the pilot to see past the TFO. Essentially, the aircraft is pirouetting overhead. This works, but the aircrew's workload will be very high, and it will be more difficult for them to stay oriented. Most of the pilot's attention will have to be focused outside 90 degrees to the left or right. This will make it more difficult for them to see hazards near the aircraft.

Searchlights sometimes enable ground units to see where an aircrew is focusing their attention, but searchlights have significant tactical drawbacks. For example, they tell the suspect that the aircrew is watching them, which oftentimes is all it takes to make them keep running. In those situations, the suspect is running from the light. When a TFO is illuminating a suspect, he/she is essentially lighting the suspect's path, while ground units are left running in the dark. Some suspects may give up out of futility, but most keep running until they are either caught or they escape. They usually do not try to hide when they are being illuminated, because they know the aircrew is watching them.

Suspects obviously know when the helicopter is overhead, but if the TFO is using FLIR, suspects do not know if the aircrew sees them. When they are not being illuminated, suspects will usually stop running and/or hide somewhere nearby if officers are not right behind them. That is exactly what an aircrew should want them to do. When a suspect stops running and hides, a very dynamic situation becomes more controllable, which significantly reduces the aircrew's workload. It is easier for pilots to orbit stationary objects and easier for both crewmembers to stay oriented. It is also much easier for a TFO to direct ground units to someone who is hiding than to someone who is running.

Figure 44 is a diagram of foot pursuit orbit profile when a searchlight is being used. Figure 45 is a diagram of a foot pursuit orbit profile when a FLIR is being used. When a FLIR is being used, the pilot can fly much higher and can position the aircraft much closer to the tactical environment. Once again, it is important to emphasize that "closer" does not mean "lower." It simply means that the aircraft's lateral offset distance from the suspect can be less than when using a searchlight.

The FLIR image at the beginning of this chapter was captured from a videotape of a foot pursuit, and a newer generation FLIR was being used. Officers were right behind the suspect, which is why he kept run-

Figure 44. This diagram represents a typical orbit profile when a searchlight is used to illuminate a suspect during a foot pursuit. The aircraft usually has to be flown lower, with a greater lateral offset distance from the suspect than when using FLIR.

ning. The suspect was not being illuminated and the helicopter was being flown at 1100 feet AGL. The FLIR symbology indicates a 30 degree down-angle on the left side of the helicopter, and the aircraft had about a 10 degree angle of bank. The pilot could not see the suspect outside the aircraft during most of the foot pursuit, because the suspect was too low in relation to the left side of the aircraft. It was very easy for the pilot to fly the mission, however, because the aircraft's altitude enabled the pilot to fly a very relaxed, high orbit over the suspect. That orbit profile also made it easier for the TFO to keep the suspect on the display. A short time later the suspect hid in a backyard when he outran the officers. This gave the aircrew time to get ground units into position around him and he was apprehended.

When aircrews are initially learning these techniques, there is a tendency for pilots to use the same orbit profile as when using a searchlight. This is not necessary, however, and is in fact undesirable. It will

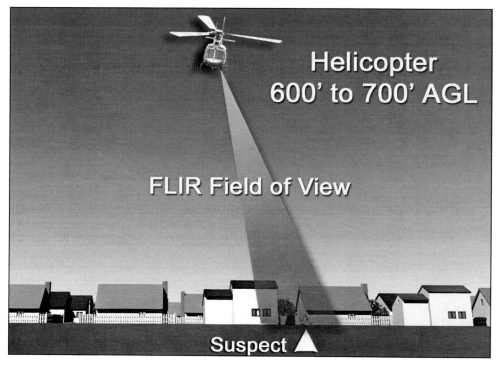

Figure 45. This diagram represents an orbit profile when a FLIR is used to watch a suspect during a foot pursuit. The aircraft can be flown much higher and closer to the suspect than when using a searchlight.

cause the aircrew's workload to increase significantly and they will lose the safety and tactical benefits of flying higher. A good orbit profile to use during nighttime foot pursuits, when the TFO is using an older generation FLIR, is to fly at approximately 30 knots, at between 600 and 700 feet AGL with a lateral offset of about of one-quarter of a city block. Newer generation FLIRs will enable an aircrew to fly even higher with the same or better results. They have much better stabilization and much higher resolution.

CONCLUSION

The advances in airborne law enforcement technology have been remarkable, but technology does not replace good law enforcement skills or judgment; it augments them. Acquiring new technology is only half the battle. Aircrews must also train with that technology to become proficient. It is ironic that that an agency would spend more than 200,000 dollars on a thermal imager, for example, yet little or nothing on training for their aircrews to become proficient.

The tactics and techniques described in this book will be familiar to some aircrews but not to others. For those who are less familiar with them, it is my sincerest hope that you will experiment with them and that you will ultimately realize the same safety and tactical benefits that we have.

Oftentimes, it is the newer people in a unit who get excited about trying something new. Sometimes, however, it can be discouraging when someone tries to wag the dog. Change can be difficult. Leadership plays an important role in inspiring and encouraging others to experiment with new ideas, but safety should always be the first consideration.

It is a quietly acknowledged fact that no one on the ground usually knows when an aircrew has screwed up a call, or when they did not find a suspect that should have been found. I have directed officers to more beehives, water-heaters, manhole covers, and mean dogs than I care to remember. I've been embarrassed at some of the mistakes that I've made that were captured on videotape for all to see, but I have learned from those mistakes. With the patience and assistance of other members in my aviation unit, and with the help of other airborne law enforcement professionals, we have been able to develop tactics that enable aircrews to operate much safer and far more effectively than ever before. Those tactics were developed with some fundamental helicopter safety principles in mind: develop good crew coordination skills, fly as high as is practical, stay proficient, and always, always, always—fly the aircraft first.

Fly safe.

INDEX

A

Acquiring objects with FLIR, 51
Adjusting the radio volumes, 18
Aircraft positioning, 56, 58, 73, 88, 97, 99
Aircrew duties during pursuits, 93

B

Binoculars, 9–10, 22, 30, 102

C

Calling the pursuit, 94
Canyon searches, 71
Centering objects in the display, 69
City blocks as references, 25, 62
Clearing intersections, 94
Cockpit obstructions, 26
Communicating with ground units, 30
Confusing heat sources, 68, 74
Confusing officers with suspects, 72
Covering officers on the street, 39
Crew qualifications, 3
Crew seating arrangements, 4
Crimes in progress,29
Crimes that just occurred, 32

D

Daytime FLIR missions, 76
Daytime orbit profiles, 24
Directing officers to armed suspects, 70
Directing officers to heat sources, 69–70
Dual monitors, 7

E

Effective radio procedures, 18
Escape routes, 33, 56
Estimating distances to suspects, 70

F

FLIR monitor placement, 6
FLIR scan tactics, 89
FLIR search patterns, 62, 75
FLIR search tactics, 63
Foot pursuits, 109–110
Forward looking infrared (FLIR), 6

G

Gunfire, shooting at aircraft, 11

H

Heat anomalies, 84, 86, 90
High profile perimeters, 71
High-rise environments, 45
High-risk traffic stops, 45
Hovering, 27, 44, 68, 102, 109
Human infrared characteristics, 51, 75

I

Infrared properties, 50
Infrared spectrum, 52
Interpreting the FLIR image, 62
Intimidating suspects, 36, 39

117

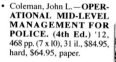
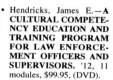